LEADERSHIP SKILLS FOR SUCCESSFUL MANAGERS

PROVEN STRATEGIES FOR MOTIVATING TEAMS AND ACHIEVING YOUR GOALS

RON LAGRONE

© **Copyright 2023 - All rights reserved.**

The content contained within this book may not be reproduced, duplicated or transmitted without direct written permission from the author or the publisher.

Under no circumstances will any blame or legal responsibility be held against the publisher, or author, for any damages, reparation, or monetary loss due to the information contained within this book. Either directly or indirectly.

Legal Notice:

This book is copyright protected. This book is only for personal use. You cannot amend, distribute, sell, use, quote or paraphrase any part, or the content within this book, without the consent of the author or publisher.

Disclaimer Notice:

Please note the information contained within this document is for educational and entertainment purposes only. All effort has been executed to present accurate, up to date, and reliable, complete information. No warranties of any kind are declared or implied. Readers acknowledge that the author is not engaging in the rendering of legal, financial, medical or professional advice. The content within this book has been derived from various sources. Please consult a licensed professional before attempting any techniques outlined in this book.

By reading this document, the reader agrees that under no circumstances is the author responsible for any losses, direct or indirect, which are incurred as a result of the use of information contained within this document, including, but not limited to, — errors, omissions, or inaccuracies.

CONTENTS

Introduction — 5

1. THE ESSENCE OF EFFECTIVE LEADERSHIP — 13
   - Defining an Effective Manager — 14
   - The Four Critical Behaviors of Leadership — 18
   - The 4 Behavioral Leadership Styles — 22
   - Balancing Management and Leadership Responsibilities — 25
   - Stories: Real-life Examples of Effective Leadership — 32

2. BUILDING STRONG RELATIONSHIPS WITH YOUR TEAM — 35
   - Getting to Know Your People through One-on-Ones — 36
   - Overcoming Resistance to One-on-Ones — 41
   - Fostering Trust and Open Communication — 53
   - Real-life Stories on Building a Relationship with Leadership — 63

3. DEVELOPING HIGH-PERFORMANCE TEAMS — 67
   - Characteristics of High-Performance Teams — 69
   - Addressing Common Team Challenges — 80
   - Team-Building Activities that Work — 87

4. MASTERING LEADERSHIP COMMUNICATION — 99
Understanding Effective Leadership Communication? — 100
The Art of Giving Feedback — 111
Encouraging effective future behavior — 121

5. EMPOWERING YOUR TEAM THROUGH COACHING AND DELEGATION — 131
The Manager Tools Delegation Model — 131
How to Start Coaching Your Team — 142
Overcoming Resistance to Delegation — 158

6. NAVIGATING CONFLICT AND CRISIS MANAGEMENT — 165
Recognizing and handling conflicts — 165
Leading through a crisis — 174
Crisis Management — 179
Post-Crisis Recovery and Lessons Learned — 199

7. DRIVING CHANGE AND ADDRESSING MODERN LEADERSHIP CHALLENGES — 207
Understanding Change Management — 207
Change leadership — 231
The Power of Adaptability: Building a Resilient Workforce — 235

8. BOOSTING SELF-CONFIDENCE AND OVERCOMING SELF-DOUBT — 247
Understanding imposter Syndrome — 247
Building self-confidence in yourself and your team — 260
Leveraging Fear for Personal and Professional Growth — 273

Conclusion — 285
References — 289

INTRODUCTION

"Great leaders are born, not made." How often have you heard this statement? It's an idea that has permeated our collective consciousness, leaving many aspiring managers feeling helpless as if they're forever destined to be average at best. Well, what if I told you that this notion is nothing more than a myth? What if I revealed the secrets of exceptional leadership skills that can be acquired, honed, and mastered? Imagine the impact you could have on your career, your team, and your organization.

A survey conducted by the Society for Human Resource Management and Logicalis, a human resources consulting firm, indicated that of 300 managers surveyed, 71% said they had unrealistic expectations of themselves. Moreover, 82% of the managers surveyed felt their leadership skills were not as effective as they should be. So where does one begin to become a better leader? As self-help manuals will tell you, "You can't become a better leader overnight." However, avoiding becoming an ineffective leader overnight is only half the battle. Numerous skills and strategies need to be mastered daily to improve the effectiveness of your leadership and management style.

The American Management Association (AMA) found that 91 percent of executives at large companies believed that management skills are learnable. A survey by the AMA and Duke University proves this to be true. In this study, researchers found that leadership can be taught to anyone at any age. They determined which factors contributed most to leadership success, using a statistical analysis of assessments by all levels of managers within forty-one large organizations.

Daily, countless managers grapple with a common set of problems and pains. Perhaps you can relate to some of them. As a reader, you have already taken the first step towards enhancing your leadership abilities by picking up this book, "Leadership Skills for Successful Managers." Within these pages lies a wealth of knowledge and practical insights that will empower you to become a highly effective and influential leader. But what led you to seek out this book in the first place?

Do you struggle to inspire and motivate your team, often facing resistance and apathy? Do you find it challenging to communicate your vision effectively, leaving your team members feeling lost and disconnected? Are you overwhelmed by the ever-changing demands of your role, constantly juggling multiple responsibilities without a clear sense of direction?

If you are familiar with any of these, you're not alone. It is not the title that caught your attention; it was the catalyst, the underlying reasons that compelled you to explore leadership skills. The desire to advance your career and secure a managerial role may have driven you here. Or perhaps you recognized the need to overcome the challenges you currently face as a leader, such as dealing with conflicts, inspiring your team, or driving sustainable results.

Regardless of the catalyst that prompted you to embark on this journey, one thing is clear: you seek a solution to the problems and pain points accompanying ineffective leadership. You understand the importance of cultivating the right skills and qualities to impact those you lead and the organizations you serve positively.

In today's fast-paced, competitive business landscape, the need for exceptional leadership skills has never been more critical. As a manager, you are expected to navigate complex challenges, drive innovation, and achieve results. Yet, the traditional notion of leadership often falls short, leaving many managers ill-equipped to rise above the mediocrity that plagues their professional lives.

So, what is the catalyst that has brought you to this book? Is it the desire to break free from the shackles of average leadership and unlock your full potential? Is it the burning ambition to make a lasting impact on your team and organization? Or perhaps it's the frustration of witnessing the consequences of ineffective leadership first-hand, knowing deep down that there must be a better way. Whatever your catalyst may be, this book is tailored to address your unique needs and aspirations.

Leadership Skills for Successful Managers is not just another self-help book. It's a transformative guide explicitly designed for ambitious managers like you who are ready to unleash their hidden leadership potential. By diving deep into the core principles of exceptional leadership, this book will equip you with the tools, strategies, and mindset necessary to elevate your managerial skills to new heights.

So, why should you invest your time and energy into reading this book? Let me reveal the benefits and shortcuts you will gain by immersing yourself in its pages. First and foremost, you will learn how to inspire and motivate your team with purpose and passion, cultivating an environment where every team member thrives. You will gain insights into effective communication techniques that will allow you to articulate your vision, align your team, and foster collaboration.

Moreover, this book will provide invaluable strategies for navigating change and uncertainty, empowering you to lead confidently and resiliently. You will discover how to leverage your strengths while developing the areas that require improvement, transforming yourself into a well-rounded and adaptable leader. Additionally, you will gain a deep understanding of emotional intelligence and how it can enhance your leadership capabilities, enabling you to navigate interpersonal dynamics and build meaningful relationships.

Beyond these immediate benefits, the wisdom imparted in this book will have a profound ripple effect on your career trajectory. As you develop and embody the principles of exceptional leadership, you will unlock doors to new opportunities and advancement. Your ability to drive results, inspire innovation, and create a positive work culture will make you an invaluable asset to your organization.

I have dealt with many aspiring managers who were frustrated with their limited success and felt besieged by "the system." They've shared their misery and anguish with me, asking if they can do anything to change things. Drawing on my experience as a leader and expert in leadership, I have witnessed first-hand the challenges that aspiring managers face. This book is designed to help you navigate the trenches of leadership, replacing mediocre efforts with exceptional skills.

I have seen super smart peers who fail to execute their ideas, and if you do not have a solid foundation, you will never be able to execute your ideas. You will learn to tune into the voice of your intuition, which, when coupled with conscious awareness, can turbocharge your leadership skills and amplify your impact. By the end of this book, you will understand that leadership is an art that requires practice and fortitude, but with commitment and passion comes greatness.

I am an authority because I have been where you are at. I have achieved what you are striving for, but I faced many challenges and overcame them using the lessons learned in this book. If you have a burning desire to become a better leader, take the challenges to grow your leadership skills and, over time, achieve greatness. If you're ready to break free from the shackles of average leadership and embark on a transformative journey toward becoming an exceptional manager, this book is your guide.

Exploring the core principles of effective leadership and providing actionable strategies will empower you to unleash your hidden potential, inspire your team, and achieve unparalleled success in your professional life. No longer will you be bound by the limitations of outdated beliefs about innate leadership abilities. Instead, you will discover that the power to become a successful manager lies within you, waiting to be unleashed.

It took me several years to figure out that I could become an outstanding leader. At first, I thought I lacked the necessary leadership skills and connections to attain greatness. But gradually, over time, my abilities began to outstrip my ego's limitations and enlightened me that my vision was far greater than I had imagined. You will become a true leader in your field by bringing these qualities with your intelligence and abilities. I've discovered that there is a formula for achieving greatness as a manager. It's not about having good communication or technical skills; it's about having all these skills but putting them into action when it matters most.

Are you ready to embark on this journey of transformation? Are you ready to redefine your role as a leader and make a lasting impact on your team and organization? If so, then take the first step and immerse yourself in the pages of Leadership Skills for Successful

Managers. Prepare to unlock the secrets of exceptional leadership and watch as your career soars to new heights.

Remember, great leaders are not simply born; they are made through continuous learning, self-reflection, and acquiring essential skills. This book is key to unlocking your full leadership potential and becoming the exceptional manager you were always meant to be. The time for average leadership is over. It's time to embrace your true capabilities and lead with confidence, purpose, and impact.

Are you ready to take the leap? The journey begins now.

CHAPTER 1
THE ESSENCE OF EFFECTIVE LEADERSHIP

A staggering 79% of employees will quit after receiving inadequate appreciation from their managers. 69% of Millennials are concerned that their workplace does not develop their leadership skills. The number of women on boards of directors is only 15%. In business, 83% of companies say developing leaders is crucial. These statistics emphasize the need for effective leadership in today's dynamic and ever-changing work environment.

Effective leadership is a critical component of a successful organization. It requires a delicate balance of management and leadership responsibilities, as well as a deep understanding of the multifaceted nature of a leader's role. In this chapter, we will explore the qualities and traits that make a manager effective, provide clear and actionable tips for aspiring managers to improve their effectiveness, and emphasize the importance of building strong relationships with team members, setting clear goals and expectations, effective communication, and demonstrating leadership through example.

DEFINING AN EFFECTIVE MANAGER

An effective manager is someone who can successfully blend management and leadership responsibilities. They are able to set goals and expectations for their team, provide support and resources, give feedback and recognition, and serve as a role model for their employees. As a manager, it's essential to understand the differences between managing and leading, recognizing that your role extends beyond being a boss to also encompass being a friend, mentor, cheerleader, and coach to your team members.

What's the Difference Between Leaders and Managers?

While the terms "leader" and "manager" are often used interchangeably, there are key differences between the two. A manager is responsible for overseeing and organizing the day-to-day operations of a team or department, ensuring that goals are met and tasks are completed on time. A leader, on the other hand, inspires and motivates others to achieve their best, sets the vision and direction for the team, and fosters a positive work culture.

What Are the Traits a Manager Must Possess?

Some essential traits that an effective manager should possess include the following:

- **Excellent communication skills:** Clear and concise communication is vital for setting expectations, providing feedback, and resolving conflicts.
- **Organization and planning abilities:** An effective manager must be able to prioritize

tasks, delegate responsibilities, and manage time effectively.
- **Flexibility:** Managers should be adaptable and willing to embrace change, as well as open to new ideas and suggestions from their team members.
- **Problem-solving skills:** Managers must be able to identify issues and develop creative solutions to address them.
- **Emotional intelligence:** Understanding and managing emotions, both your own and those of your team members, is crucial for building strong relationships and fostering a positive work environment.

What Are the Traits a Leader Possesses?

In addition to the traits mentioned above, effective leaders also exhibit the following qualities:

- **Vision:** Leaders set a clear direction for their team and communicate this vision effectively.
- **Empathy:** Understanding and connecting with team members on a personal level helps to build trust and rapport.
- **Resilience:** Leaders must be able to bounce back from setbacks and remain focused on achieving their goals.

- **Integrity:** A leader's honesty, ethics, and transparency are essential for building trust and credibility within their team.
- **Inspirational:** Effective leaders motivate and inspire their team members to strive for excellence and reach their full potential.

How to Measure Effective Leadership and Management?

Measuring the effectiveness of leadership and management can be done through various methods, such as employee satisfaction surveys, performance reviews, and observing team dynamics. Regular feedback from team members can provide valuable insights into a manager's strengths and areas for improvement.

11 Traits You Need to Be a Highly Effective Leader

To be a highly effective leader, you should strive to embody the following traits:

- Excellent communication skills
- Organization and planning abilities
- Flexibility
- Problem-solving skills
- Emotional intelligence
- Vision

- Empathy
- Resilience
- Integrity
- Inspirational
- Continuous personal and professional growth

By developing and honing these traits, you can transform yourself into the kind of leader your team will respect and admire. As you progress on your leadership journey, remember that effective leadership is an ongoing process that requires continuous self-reflection, learning, and adaptation.

THE FOUR CRITICAL BEHAVIORS OF LEADERSHIP

To lead their teams to success, effective leaders must exhibit four critical behaviors. These behaviors include setting clear expectations and goals, providing ongoing support and coaching, encouraging open communication and collaboration, and holding themselves and their team accountable for achieving results. In this section, we will discuss each of these behaviors in detail, providing real-world examples and practical tips for how you can develop and implement them in your leadership style. We will also highlight the consequences of ineffective leadership behaviors, demonstrating the importance of mastering these critical behaviors for long-term success as a leader.

Setting Clear Expectations and Goals

One of the essential responsibilities of a leader is to set clear expectations and goals for their team. This involves defining objectives, establishing priorities, and ensuring that everyone understands their role and responsibilities. By setting clear expectations, leaders empower their team members to take ownership of their work and stay focused on achieving the desired outcomes.

Practical tips for setting clear expectations and goals include:

- Communicate your vision and objectives to your team, ensuring everyone understands the overall direction and desired outcomes.
- Break down larger goals into smaller, achievable tasks and milestones.
- Regularly review progress and adjust goals as needed based on feedback and changing circumstances.

Providing Ongoing Support and Coaching

Effective leaders recognize the importance of providing ongoing support and coaching to their team members. This involves offering guidance, encouragement, and resources to help individuals develop their skills and overcome challenges. By acting as a coach and mentor, leaders can foster a growth mindset within their team and create a culture of continuous improvement.

Practical tips for providing ongoing support and coaching include:

- Invest time in getting to know your team members, and understanding their strengths, weaknesses, and aspirations.
- Offer regular feedback, both positive and constructive, to help team members grow and improve.
- Encourage and facilitate professional development opportunities, such as training courses, workshops, and conferences.

Encouraging Open Communication and Collaboration

Open communication and collaboration are crucial for effective teamwork and innovation. Leaders should create an environment where team members feel comfortable sharing their ideas, opinions, and concerns. By fostering a culture of transparency and trust, leaders can ensure that everyone's voice is heard and that the best ideas are brought forward.

Practical tips for encouraging open communication and collaboration include:

- Establish regular team meetings and check-ins to discuss progress, challenges, and new ideas.
- Create a safe space for open and honest dialogue, encouraging team members to express their thoughts without fear of judgment or reprisal.
- Actively listen to feedback and suggestions, demonstrating your commitment to continuous improvement and teamwork.

Holding Themselves and Their Team Accountable

Accountability is a crucial aspect of effective leadership. Leaders must hold themselves and their team members responsible for achieving results and meeting expectations. By setting clear goals, providing support and coaching, and fostering open communication, leaders can create an environment where everyone understands their responsibilities and is committed to delivering results.

Practical tips for holding yourself and your team accountable include:

- Clearly communicate expectations and responsibilities, ensuring everyone understands their role in achieving the team's goals.
- Regularly review progress and address any performance issues promptly and constructively.
- Recognize and celebrate successes, reinforcing the importance of accountability and the value of hard work.

THE 4 BEHAVIORAL LEADERSHIP STYLES

There are various leadership styles, each with its strengths and weaknesses. The four behavioral leadership styles include directive, supportive, participative, and achievement-oriented leadership:

Directive Leadership: This style involves providing clear instructions and closely supervising tasks to ensure they are completed correctly and on time. Directive leaders often make decisions without seeking input from their team.

Supportive Leadership: Supportive leaders prioritize the well-being and development of their team members. They are approachable, empathetic, and focused on creating a positive and inclusive work environment.

Participative Leadership: Participative leaders involve their team members in decision-making and problem-solving processes, valuing their input and expertise. This style fosters a sense of collaboration and ownership among team members.

Achievement-Oriented Leadership: Achievement-oriented leaders set ambitious goals and encourage their teams to strive for excellence. They provide the necessary support and resources to help team members reach their full potential.

The Ideal Leadership Style

The most effective leadership style often depends on the specific situation and the unique needs of your team. As a leader, it's crucial to adapt your approach to best support and empower your team members. The ideal leadership style is often a combination of the four behavioral styles, striking a balance between providing clear direction, offering support and encouragement, fostering collaboration, and setting high expectations for performance.

What is an Ineffective Leader?

An ineffective leader is one who fails to exhibit the four critical behaviors of leadership, often resulting in a lack of direction, disengaged team members, and poor performance. Ineffective leaders may struggle with communication, fail to provide adequate support and guidance, or lack accountability for their actions and decisions.

Examples of ineffective leaders include:

- Leaders who micromanage their team stifling creativity and autonomy.
- Leaders who avoid making difficult decisions or addressing performance issues.
- Leaders who prioritize their personal goals and interests over the needs and well-being of their team.

Exhibiting the four critical behaviors of leadership is essential for becoming an effective leader. By setting clear expectations and goals, providing ongoing support and coaching, encouraging open communication and collaboration, and holding yourself and your team accountable for achieving results, you can create a supportive and successful work environment.

As you strive to develop and refine these behaviors, remember that the most effective leadership style is often a combination of the four behavioral styles tailored to the unique needs of your team and the specific challenges you face.

BALANCING MANAGEMENT AND LEADERSHIP RESPONSIBILITIES

To excel as a leader and a manager, it is crucial to strike the right balance between the roles and responsibilities associated with each. This involves delegating tasks, motivating team members, setting goals, and making decisions. Finding the right balance between management and leadership skills is vital for success in any organization.

What is Leadership?

Leadership is the ability to guide, inspire, and influence others toward achieving a common goal. It involves creating a vision for the future, setting a strategic direction, and empowering team members to contribute their best efforts. A leader fosters a positive work environment that encourages collaboration, innovation, and continuous improvement.

Roles and Responsibilities of a Leader

A leader has numerous roles and responsibilities, including:

- Setting a vision and defining a clear direction for the team
- Inspiring and motivating team members to achieve their potential
- Fostering a collaborative and supportive work environment
- Empowering team members to take ownership of their tasks and responsibilities
- Providing guidance, mentorship, and coaching to team members
- Encouraging open communication and feedback
- Making strategic decisions that align with organizational goals

How to Become a Leader?

Becoming a leader involves developing key skills such as emotional intelligence, effective communication, strategic thinking, and adaptability. It also requires a genuine commitment to personal and professional growth, as well as a willingness to learn from mistakes and challenges. To become a leader, one must actively seek opportunities to lead, practice leadership skills, and continually refine their approach based on feedback and self-reflection.

Leadership vs. Management: How to Strike the Right Balance in Your Business

Soft Skills Count

While management skills are critical for organizing and coordinating resources, soft skills such as empathy, active listening, and emotional intelligence are equally important for effective leadership. Developing soft skills can enhance your ability to connect with your team and understand their needs, ultimately leading to a more cohesive and high-performing team.

It's not either-or: Management and Leadership Go Hand-in-Hand.

Management and leadership are not mutually exclusive; they are complementary skill sets that contribute to a successful team. A well-rounded manager will combine strong management skills, such as planning, organizing, and monitoring performance, with leadership qualities like vision, inspiration, and adaptability. This balance enables managers to effectively guide their teams through challenges and towards success.

How to Balance Leadership and Management

- To strike the right balance between leadership and management, consider the following strategies:
- Clearly define your role as both a leader and a manager and understand the unique responsibilities associated with each.
- Assess your strengths and weaknesses in both leadership and management skills and develop a plan for improvement.
- Allocate time for both strategic thinking and day-to-day management tasks.
- Practice active listening and open communication to build strong relationships with your team members.
- Empower your team by delegating tasks, providing resources, and offering support when needed.
- Continuously learn and adapt your leadership style based on feedback and changing circumstances.

Finding the Balance between Management and Leadership

Striking the right balance between management and leadership is essential for managers who aspire to create a thriving, high-performing work environment. It requires a deep understanding of the unique roles and responsibilities associated with each and a commitment to developing and refining the skills necessary for success. Here are some practical steps you can take to find the balance between management and leadership.

Self-Assessment

Begin by conducting a thorough self-assessment to identify your strengths and weaknesses in both management and leadership skills. Be honest with yourself and consider seeking feedback from colleagues or mentors to gain a comprehensive understanding of your abilities. Reflect on your past experiences and identify areas where you excelled and areas that need improvement.

Personal Development Plan

Create a personal development plan that focuses on strengthening your weaknesses and enhancing your strengths. This plan should include actionable steps, such as attending workshops, reading books, seeking mentorship, or engaging in online courses. Regularly review and update your development plan to track your progress and ensure that you continue to grow as a leader and manager.

Time Management

Effective time management is crucial for balancing management and leadership responsibilities. Allocate time for strategic thinking and long-term planning, as well as for addressing day-to-day management tasks. Utilize tools and techniques such as time-blocking, prioritization, and delegation to ensure that you can effectively manage your time and responsibilities.

Build Strong Relationships

Developing strong relationships with your team members is an essential aspect of both management and leadership. Practice active listening and open communication to foster trust and rapport with your team. Empathize with their concerns and provide support and guidance when needed. By building strong relationships, you can better understand your team's needs and tailor your leadership approach accordingly.

Empower Your Team

Empowering your team is a crucial aspect of finding the balance between management and leadership. Delegate tasks to your team members and provide them with the autonomy and resources they need to succeed. Encourage creativity and innovation and create a supportive environment where team members feel comfortable taking risks and exploring new ideas.

Adaptability

The ability to adapt and evolve your leadership style based on changing circumstances and feedback is critical for finding the right balance between management and leadership. Continuously evaluate your approach and adjust as needed, considering the unique needs and dynamics of your team and organization. Be open to learning from your experiences and embrace the growth that comes with change.

Celebrate Success and Learn from Failure

Recognize and celebrate your team's successes and use failures as learning opportunities. This approach fosters a positive work environment where team members feel valued and motivated to continuously improve. By acknowledging achievements and addressing setbacks constructively, you can demonstrate your commitment to both management and leadership.

Finding the balance between management and leadership is an ongoing process that requires self-awareness, personal growth, and adaptability. By following these practical steps and continuously refining your skills, you can create a work environment that fosters success, innovation, and teamwork. As you strike the right balance between management and leadership, you will inspire and guide your team to achieve their full potential and contribute to the overall success of your organization.

STORIES: REAL-LIFE EXAMPLES OF EFFECTIVE LEADERSHIP

In this section, we will share real-life stories that illustrate the principles of effective leadership discussed throughout this chapter. These stories provide valuable insights and lessons that can help you develop and refine your leadership skills.

Story 1: A Transformation in Leadership

In a Reddit post, a software development team lead shared their journey towards becoming a more effective leader. Initially, the team lead struggled with micromanagement, failing to provide clear direction, and not involving team members in decision-making processes. Over time, the team became disengaged, and productivity suffered.

The team lead decided to seek advice from mentors and invest in leadership development resources. They started implementing changes, such as setting clear expectations, fostering open communication, and involving team members in problem-solving and decision-making. As a result, the team's engagement and performance significantly improved. This story demonstrates the importance of self-awareness, continuous learning, and adaptability in leadership.

Story 2: Supporting an Employee in Need of Improvement

In a blog post by Avdi Grimm, a software developer, he shared his experience as an employee who needed improvement. Avdi described how his manager played a critical role in helping him get back on track by providing support, coaching, and encouragement. Instead of focusing on his shortcomings, the manager took a constructive approach, identifying areas where Avdi could improve and offering guidance and resources to help him develop the necessary skills.

The manager also created an environment where Avdi felt comfortable discussing his challenges and seeking help. This supportive and collaborative atmosphere ultimately led to Avdi's personal and professional growth, highlighting the importance of a leader who acts as a mentor and coach.

Chapter Summary and Key Takeaways

In this chapter, we have discussed the essence of effective leadership, including the four critical behaviors that leaders must exhibit to lead their teams to success: setting clear expectations and goals, providing ongoing support and coaching, encouraging open communication and collaboration, and holding themselves and their team accountable for achieving results.

We have also explored the different behavioral leadership styles and shared real-life stories that illustrate the power of effective leadership. By embracing these principles and continuously striving for personal and professional growth, you can become the kind of leader your team will respect and admire.

In the next chapter, we will delve deeper into the importance of building strong relationships with your team members. This includes fostering trust, empathy, and emotional intelligence, as well as leveraging effective communication strategies to create a positive and collaborative work environment. By mastering these skills, you can further enhance your leadership abilities and empower your team to achieve their full potential.

CHAPTER 2
BUILDING STRONG RELATIONSHIPS WITH YOUR TEAM

The foundation of exceptional leadership is rooted in the quality of relationships a leader establishes with their team. The second chapter, "Building Strong Relationships with Your Team," underlines this concept and emphasizes the importance of cultivating strong, meaningful connections with each team member.

As Michael Jordan once said, "Talent wins games, but teamwork and intelligence win championships." This statement underscores that while individual abilities are important, it's the strength of relationships within the team and the collective intelligence that truly brings success.

GETTING TO KNOW YOUR PEOPLE THROUGH ONE-ON-ONES

The one-on-one meeting, a powerful tool for building strong relationships with team members, offers a platform for personal engagement and collaboration. These meetings not only help in understanding the aspirations, challenges, and thoughts of individual team members, but also allow leaders to share their own perspectives, thus fostering a two-way communication channel. One-on-one meetings serve as a significant cornerstone for transparent conversations, building trust, and enhancing overall team performance.

One-on-one meetings: A comprehensive guide for managers and employees

In these meetings, the spotlight is on the individual. Both managers and employees should approach one-on-ones with an open mind, readiness to learn and share, and commitment to follow-up actions. The primary goal is to promote a deeper understanding between managers and employees, thus fueling a collaborative working relationship.

What are one-on-one meetings, and why should you have them?

One-on-one meetings are scheduled, recurring meetings between a manager and an individual team member. They provide a forum for ongoing feedback, career development, personal engagement, and alignment around performance and expectations. By facilitating these meetings, managers can learn more about their team members, address concerns or roadblocks, provide constructive feedback, and develop stronger relationships.

How should managers and employees approach one-on-one meetings?

One-on-one meetings should be approached as a collaborative conversation rather than a status update. Both parties should come prepared with talking points, and managers should ensure the focus is on the employee. They should be an open dialogue, with both parties actively listening, providing feedback, and being open to new ideas and perspectives.

Who owns the one-on-one meeting?

While managers often schedule one-on-one meetings, it's essential to understand that these meetings are for the benefit of the employee. Thus, the ownership of the meeting should ideally be with the employee. They should feel empowered to bring up any topic, concern, or idea that they believe is important.

What do you talk about in a one-on-one?

The topics discussed in one-on-one meetings can vary greatly depending on the needs of the team member and the immediate context of the work environment. It can range from project updates, performance feedback, career aspirations, learning and development opportunities, or even personal life events that may impact work.

How to have an effective one-on-one meeting & One-on-one meeting template

Having an effective one-on-one meeting involves preparation, active listening, asking open-ended questions, providing and receiving feedback, and setting up follow-up actions. Using a meeting template can help structure the conversation and ensure that all important areas are covered. The template might include sections for personal updates, feedback and recognition, current projects and challenges, career development, and follow-up actions.

Take time to make time: Before the meeting & The heart of the meeting

Prioritizing one-on-one meetings and setting aside dedicated time for them underscores their importance. Before the meeting, both parties should prepare for the discussion, bringing up any topics, questions, or feedback they want to cover. The heart of the meeting should be a productive dialogue, where both parties feel heard and valued, leading to action items or insights.

The benefits of 1-on-b1 meetings

The benefits of one-on-one meetings are manifold, impacting both individuals and the team as a whole, and thereby influencing the overall health and success of an organization.

Promote Clear Communication: One-on-one meetings offer a platform for direct, candid, and clear communication. Both the manager and the employee can share updates, concerns, ideas, or feedback in an open, focused dialogue, reducing the risk of miscommunication.

Build Strong Relationships: These meetings foster a better understanding and rapport between managers and employees.

Facilitate Problem-Solving: One-on-one meetings can provide a safe space to surface and discuss problems, challenges, or concerns that an employee may be facing.

Boost Employee Engagement and Morale: By dedicating time and attention to each team member, managers show that they value and care about their employees as individuals, not just as workers. This can significantly increase employee engagement and morale.

Enhance Performance: One-on-one meetings allow for ongoing feedback, both praise for a job well done and constructive criticism to improve performance. Such regular feedback can lead to continuous improvement and enhanced performance.

Align Goals: These meetings are an excellent opportunity for aligning personal career goals with organizational objectives, ensuring that everyone is working toward the same vision.

3 common pitfalls of 1-on-1 meetings

While one-on-one meetings offer myriad benefits, there can be common pitfalls that might undermine their effectiveness if not properly addressed. Being aware of these potential issues is the first step to ensuring productive and fruitful one-on-one sessions.

1. Lack of Preparation: One common pitfall is going into a one-on-one meeting without proper preparation. Preparation is key to effective meetings; without it, the meeting can easily become unproductive, unfocused, and a waste of time.

2. Dominated by Manager: A one-on-one meeting is not a platform for managers to deliver lengthy monologues or provide unidirectional feedback. If a manager dominates the conversation, the employee might feel unheard or unimportant.

3. Treating Meetings as a Checkbox Activity: Some managers treat one-on-ones as a routine, mundane task to be ticked off, rather than a strategic opportunity to engage with and develop their team members.

Navigating these pitfalls requires thoughtful intention and active engagement from both the manager and the employee. By avoiding these common missteps, one-on-one meetings can serve as a powerful tool for building strong relationships, fostering open communication, and promoting individual and team success.

OVERCOMING RESISTANCE TO ONE-ON-ONES

The one-on-one meeting is an essential tool in the managerial toolkit, facilitating open and direct communication, relationship building, and performance feedback. However, not all employees are comfortable or enthusiastic about participating in these meetings. Resistance may stem from various factors, such as feeling unprepared, fearing criticism, misunderstanding the purpose of these meetings, or simply disliking the formal meeting format. As a manager, understanding these concerns and addressing them strategically can significantly improve participation and the overall effectiveness of one-on-one meetings.

Strategies for Encouraging Participation in One-on-One Meetings

When dealing with resistance to one-on-one meetings, the first step is to address the root cause of this resistance. Once the source of reluctance has been identified, managers can utilize specific strategies to encourage and foster active participation.

Clarify the Purpose and Benefits: Often, employees might resist one-on-one meetings because they don't understand their purpose or how they stand to benefit from them. As a manager, take the time to explain the objectives of the meetings and how they contribute to individual development and team success.

Create a Safe Environment: For open and honest communication to occur, employees need to feel safe.

Cultivate a non-judgmental space where employees feel comfortable discussing their thoughts, ideas, feelings, and concerns. Assure them that these meetings are not just about pointing out shortcomings, but also recognizing achievements and looking for opportunities for growth.

Encourage Preparation: Another source of resistance could be feeling unprepared for the meeting. Encourage employees to prepare for one-on-ones by thinking about what they'd like to discuss, jotting down any questions or concerns they might have, and reflecting on their progress and challenges since the last meeting.

Personalize Meetings: Tailor one-on-one meetings to individual employee's needs, preferences, and work styles. Some employees may prefer a more structured format, while others might appreciate a more informal, conversational approach.

Invite Feedback: Ask for feedback on the meetings. Do they find them useful? Are there aspects they'd like to change? Inviting feedback shows that you value their opinions and are willing to adjust to make the meetings more effective and beneficial for both of you.

Understanding Employee Resistance to One-on-One Meetings

When faced with resistance to one-on-one meetings, managers need to explore the underlying reasons for this resistance. Only by addressing these root causes can a solution be found to encourage participation and engagement in these important meetings.

Discomfort with One-on-One Meetings

For some employees, one-on-one meetings may evoke feelings of discomfort or unease, particularly if they have had negative experiences with such meetings in the past. It could be perceived as an opportunity for critique rather than constructive feedback, leaving employees on edge. To mitigate this, managers can emphasize the purpose of these meetings as being a supportive, constructive conversation about personal and professional development, and not a setting for harsh criticism. A relaxed, positive demeanor from the manager can also go a long way in putting an employee at ease.

Feeling Unprepared

If an employee feels unprepared for a one-on-one meeting, they may resist or dread it. To assist in this regard, managers can provide a clear agenda before the meeting, highlighting the points of discussion. This can help employees prepare their thoughts and feedback, making them more comfortable during the meeting.

Perceived Lack of Time

Employees might feel too overwhelmed with their tasks to "waste" time in a one-on-one meeting. Managers should communicate the value and purpose of these meetings, emphasizing that they are designed to support, not hinder, an employee's work.

Fear of Feedback

Some employees might resist one-on-one meetings due to a fear of negative feedback. It's important for managers to approach feedback in a constructive manner, highlighting the purpose of feedback as a tool for growth and improvement.

Misalignment with Personal Communication Style

Not everyone prefers the same style of communication. Some employees may be more comfortable with group meetings, emails, or instant messages. While it's essential to respect personal preferences, it's equally important to emphasize the unique benefits of one-on-one meetings, such as personalized feedback and deeper, more focused discussions.

By understanding these causes of resistance, managers can tailor their approach to each employee's concerns, creating an environment in which one-on-one meetings are perceived as beneficial rather than threatening. In the next section, we'll provide tips on how to make these meetings more engaging and productive.

Addressing Challenges in One-on-One Meetings

Various challenges may arise during one-on-one meetings, including disengagement and lack of participation. As a leader, you must devise effective strategies to engage your team members actively, address their concerns, and foster a productive dialogue.

Managing Disengagement

Disengagement during one-on-one meetings can be a telling sign that an employee is not invested in the process. This disengagement can manifest in several ways, such as short or non-specific answers, a lack of enthusiasm, or even frequent absences from scheduled meetings.

Create a safe space: Encourage your team members to share their thoughts openly without the fear of criticism. Assure them that these meetings are confidential and intended for their development and growth.

Discuss topics of interest: If the team member is disinterested in the conversation, try to steer it towards topics they care about. Discuss their career aspirations, their current challenges, or even their interests outside of work.

Positive reinforcement: Recognize and appreciate the employee's contributions during the meeting. This not only validates their efforts but also encourages further participation.

Addressing Lack of Participation

If an employee is silent or not contributing much during meetings, it could be due to various reasons such as confusion about the meeting's purpose, feeling unheard, or simply not knowing what to say.

Set a clear agenda: By setting a clear agenda before the meeting, employees know what to expect and can prepare accordingly.

Encourage dialogue: Instead of a monologue, transform the meeting into a two-way dialogue. Ask open-ended questions that encourage the employee to share their thoughts.

Active listening: Show your interest in their opinions by actively listening to what they are saying. Respond appropriately and provide constructive feedback, which lets them know that their input is valued.

Leveraging Insights to Overcome Resistance

Insights from various sources provide valuable strategies for managers to overcome resistance and build stronger relationships with their employees through effective one-on-one meetings. These resources, grounded in research and best practices, offer a wealth of knowledge that managers can apply in their own interactions.

Understanding Resistance: Before overcoming resistance, managers must understand its root causes. Insights from sources highlight common reasons for resistance, including fear of criticism, lack of clarity about the meeting's purpose, or feelings of discomfort or unpreparedness. By recognizing these factors, managers can create more effective strategies to address them.

Adapting to Individual Needs: Each employee is unique, with their own preferences, communication styles, and comfort levels. Insights from research stress the importance of adapting one-on-one meetings to individual needs. For instance, some employees might prefer a more structured meeting, while others might thrive in a more casual, conversation-like setting.

Building Trust: Trust is crucial for effective one-on-one meetings. Insights provide actionable strategies for building trust, such as being open and transparent, showing empathy and understanding, and consistently following through on commitments.

Maintaining Consistency: Consistency plays a significant role in overcoming resistance. Regular one-on-one meetings show employees that their thoughts and opinions are valued consistently, not just once or twice.

Using Effective Communication Strategies: Good communication is key to effective one-on-one meetings. Insights provide practical advice on communication strategies, such as active listening, asking open-ended questions, and providing constructive feedback.

Five Things to Stop Doing in Employee One-on-One Meetings (and What to Start Doing!)

- Stop ignoring employee input: Start listening actively and attentively, encouraging employees to share their ideas and feedback.
- Stop focusing solely on work: Start discussing personal development, career goals, and overall wellbeing.

- Stop avoiding difficult conversations: Start addressing challenges and issues directly and constructively.
- Stop being unprepared: Start planning for the meeting ahead of time, setting a clear agenda and objectives.
- Stop dominating the conversation: Start promoting a balanced dialogue, ensuring both parties have ample opportunity to speak.

Types of Difficult People in the Workplace

Various types of difficult people may be found in a workplace:

- The Constant Complainers: Always unhappy and often spreading negativity.
- The Silent Types: They don't communicate or share information willingly.
- The Critic: Always finds something wrong but rarely offers solutions.
- The Know-it-all: Believes they are always right and dismisses others' ideas.

Nine Strategies for Managing Difficult Employees

- Have a private, direct conversation about the issue.
- Set clear expectations and consequences.
- Provide regular feedback.
- Document everything.
- Encourage improvement and provide support.
- Seek advice from HR or other leaders.
- Consider training or development programs.
- If necessary, consider reassignment or termination.
- Always treat them with respect and professionalism.

What Causes Employee Disengagement?

Employee disengagement can stem from a variety of sources:

- Lack of clarity or purpose in their role.
- Absence of recognition or reward for hard work.
- Limited opportunities for growth and development.
- Poor leadership or management.
- Lack of trust or open communication.

Identify Your Disengaged Employees

Identifying disengaged employees involves noticing changes in behavior such as decreased productivity, increased absenteeism, less participation in meetings or discussions, and negative attitudes towards work.

Determine the Impact of Disengaged Employees

Disengaged employees can significantly impact an organization, including decreased productivity, lower customer satisfaction, increased turnover rates, and a negative influence on team morale.

How to Handle Disengaged Employees

Handling disengaged employees involves understanding the root of their disengagement, having open and honest conversations about their feelings, and creating an action plan to improve their engagement.

How to Re-engage Disengaged Employees

Re-engaging disengaged employees can be achieved by:

- Providing clear and meaningful goals.
- Offering opportunities for growth and development.

- Recognizing and appreciating their work.
- Promoting a healthy work-life balance.
- Fostering an open and trusting environment.

Why Do Employees Hate Meetings, And What Can Be Done to Make Them Better?

Employees often dislike meetings because they may seem unproductive, too long, lacking clear objectives, or they interfere with their work. To make meetings better:

- Set a clear agenda and stick to it.
- Keep meetings short and to the point.
- Only involve relevant parties.
- Encourage participation and feedback.
- Follow up with clear action points and assignments.

FOSTERING TRUST AND OPEN COMMUNICATION

Communication is the lifeblood of any organization. It enables a free flow of ideas, encourages collaboration, and ensures everyone is working towards the same goals. As a leader, fostering trust and open communication in your team or organization is a critical aspect of effective leadership.

The Importance of Fostering Trust and Open Communication

Creates a Collaborative Environment

When there's trust and open communication in a team, it promotes a collaborative environment. Employees feel comfortable sharing their ideas, feedback, and concerns without fear of judgment or backlash. This leads to a free exchange of ideas, stimulating innovation, and problem-solving.

Boosts Employee Engagement and Morale

Trust and open communication help to boost employee engagement and morale. When employees feel trusted, they are more likely to take ownership of their work and be proactive in their roles. They are also more likely to feel valued and recognized, contributing to higher job satisfaction and lower turnover rates.

Promotes Transparency

Open communication promotes transparency within an organization. Leaders who communicate openly about the organization's goals, strategies, challenges, and achievements help employees understand their roles within the larger framework. This helps to align individual goals with organizational goals, contributing to better performance and productivity.

Improves Decision-Making

Trust and open communication contribute to better decision-making within an organization. When there's open communication, information flows freely, leading to better-informed decisions.

Trust, on the other hand, enables leaders to delegate tasks and decision-making responsibilities, empowering employees and leading to faster, more efficient decision-making.

Resolves Conflicts

In any organization, conflicts are inevitable. Open communication is key to effective conflict resolution. It allows issues to be discussed openly, ensuring everyone's viewpoints are considered, and mutually agreeable solutions are found. Trust, on the other hand, ensures that conflicts are addressed in a fair and respectful manner, helping to maintain positive relationships within the team.

In the subsequent sections of this chapter, we will delve deeper into these points, providing practical tips and strategies to foster trust and open communication within your team or organization. We will also highlight the consequences of a lack of trust and open communication, emphasizing the importance of these elements in creating a successful, high-performing team.

Common Communication Barriers and How to Overcome Them

Effective communication is the backbone of successful teams and organizations. However, communication doesn't always flow smoothly. Certain barriers can disrupt communication, leading to misunderstandings, conflicts, and reduced productivity. Below are some common communication barriers and how leaders can overcome them:

Cultural Differences

In multicultural teams, cultural differences can become communication barriers. Variations in language, non-verbal cues, and social customs can lead to misunderstandings.

Overcoming Cultural Differences: Encourage cultural awareness in your team. Provide diversity and inclusion training to help team members understand and respect cultural differences. Facilitate open discussions about culture and communication styles.

Technological Challenges

With remote work becoming more common, technology is a crucial communication tool. However, technology failures or lack of proficiency can hinder effective communication.

Overcoming Technological Challenges: Provide necessary technology training to all team members. Ensure that everyone has access to the tools they need to communicate effectively. Have backup plans in case of technical issues.

Physical Distractions

Noise, lack of privacy, interruptions, and other physical distractions can disrupt communication.

Overcoming Physical Distractions: Create a conducive environment for communication. Encourage respectful behavior like muting phones during meetings and maintaining quiet spaces for conversations.

Emotional Barriers

Personal feelings, biases, and preconceptions can hinder open and honest communication. People might withhold information, misinterpret messages, or shut down communication entirely.

Overcoming Emotional Barriers: Encourage emotional intelligence in your team. Foster an environment of respect and trust where team members feel safe expressing their feelings and concerns. Be aware of your own emotions and how they may affect your communication.

Lack of Clarity

Vague messages, complex jargon, or lack of context can lead to confusion and misunderstandings.

Overcoming Lack of Clarity: Ensure all communication is clear, concise, and to the point. Use simple language and provide enough context for understanding. Encourage team members to ask questions if they need clarification.

Information Overload

Too much information at once can overwhelm team members, making it hard for them to absorb important details.

Overcoming Information Overload: Break down complex information into manageable chunks. Prioritize and sequence information effectively. Use visual aids to help convey complex ideas.

The Value of Communication, Trust Building, and Enabling Open Communication

Why Communications?

Communication is vital in every aspect of life, and it is no different in a team or organization. Communication allows us to share ideas, build relationships, and collaborate effectively. In a business context, it ensures everyone is aligned with the organizational goals and understands their role in achieving them.

Building Trust, Creating Value

Trust is an essential component of any successful relationship, including those within a business environment. Building trust creates value in several ways. For example, it encourages open communication, facilitates collaboration, and promotes a positive work environment. In the long run, it can lead to increased productivity and employee satisfaction.

Making It Happen

Building trust and encouraging open communication won't happen overnight. It requires consistent effort, time, and patience. Leaders can make it happen by being transparent, showing empathy, demonstrating integrity, and being open to feedback.

The Value of Trust

Trust in an organization not only promotes a healthy work environment but also plays a pivotal role in its success. It fosters collaboration, enhances productivity, and improves employee morale. Trusting relationships also provide the stability necessary for innovation and risk-taking.

Examples of Open Communication

Open communication can take many forms in an organization:

- Regular team meetings where everyone is encouraged to speak their mind.
- One-on-one meetings between team members and managers.
- Anonymous feedback or suggestion systems.

- Open-door policies encouraging employees to speak directly with management.

Why is Open Communication Important?

Open communication is important as it leads to better decision-making, increased trust, and a more inclusive workplace environment. It ensures everyone's ideas and opinions are heard and valued, promotes transparency, and helps to address issues before they become major problems.

How to Encourage Open Communication

Leaders can encourage open communication by creating a safe and supportive environment where everyone feels free to express their thoughts and ideas without fear of retribution. This can be achieved by showing respect for all opinions, practicing active listening, and encouraging feedback.

How to Maintain Open Communication

Maintaining open communication requires consistent effort and commitment from all team members. Regular check-ins, open and honest feedback, and ensuring everyone has a voice are all crucial aspects of maintaining open communication.

7 Ways to Encourage Open Communication

- Foster a culture of respect and inclusivity.
- Ensure everyone feels safe to voice their thoughts and ideas.
- Practice active listening.
- Encourage regular feedback.
- Lead by example.
- Regularly communicate organizational goals and changes.
- Provide various communication channels.

Benefits of Open Communication

- Open communication leads to a range of benefits such as:
- Increased employee engagement and job satisfaction.
- Enhanced team collaboration.
- Better problem-solving and decision-making.
- Greater innovation due to the exchange of diverse ideas.
- Improved organizational performance.

REAL-LIFE STORIES ON BUILDING A RELATIONSHIP WITH LEADERSHIP

Story 1: The Power of Open Communication

This story is from a Reddit user who shared their experiences in the Product Management subreddit about building relationships with leadership.

The user narrated how they were initially apprehensive about voicing their ideas and concerns to the senior leadership. Over time, however, they decided to adopt a more open communication approach. They started sharing their insights and perspectives on various projects during meetings, even if they contradicted the viewpoints of some of the senior leaders.

To their surprise, instead of facing backlash, they received appreciation for their fresh perspective. The leaders valued their insights and constructive criticism. This allowed them to feel more comfortable expressing their thoughts in the future, fostering a stronger relationship with the leadership.

This story highlights the importance of open communication in building relationships with leadership. By being willing to express their views honestly and constructively, the Reddit user was able to establish trust and respect with the leaders in their organization.

Story 2: The Challenge of Leadership

In the second story, shared on the small business subreddit, a small business owner shared their struggles with feeling adequate as a leader. They felt overwhelmed by their responsibilities and doubted their capability to lead effectively.

One day, they decided to share their concerns with their team. Instead of perceiving it as a sign of weakness, the team appreciated their transparency. They were able to offer suggestions and support, which helped the business owner feel less isolated.

This story reinforces the value of trust and open communication in leadership. By sharing their vulnerabilities, the business owner was able to strengthen their relationship with their team. The team felt more connected and committed to their leader because they saw them as a human who also had challenges and doubts.

Both of these stories emphasize the critical role of open communication in building and strengthening relationships with leadership. By being open and honest, leaders can foster a culture of trust and collaboration, which benefits everyone in the organization.

Chapter Summary and Segue into Next Chapter

In this chapter, we've explored the critical importance of fostering trust and open communication within a team or organization. We've seen how these components are foundational to effective leadership and a thriving organizational culture. We've discussed the tangible benefits of building trust and encouraging open communication, including improved team morale, increased productivity, and enhanced employee engagement. In understanding the barriers to communication, we've also provided some practical tips and strategies to overcome these, thus facilitating a more open and transparent work environment.

Real-life stories have further underlined these principles, showing how leaders who embrace open communication and actively build trust can greatly improve their relationships within the team.

As we've learned, trust and open communication are not mere buzzwords but are critical elements that drive success and growth in any organization. However, these elements do not exist in isolation. They play a crucial role in forming high-performing teams, which will be the focus of our next chapter.

In the next chapter, we will delve deeper into how to cultivate a team that is not only effective but excels in what they do. We'll examine how trust and open communication, along with other factors such as team cohesion, conflict resolution, and a shared sense of purpose, contribute to the creation and sustenance of high-performing teams. Stay tuned for a journey into the mechanisms that drive team performance and success!

CHAPTER 3
DEVELOPING HIGH-PERFORMANCE TEAMS

> "If your ship doesn't come in, swim out to meet it."
>
> JONATHAN WINTERS

Creating high-performance teams is a vital task that is far from easy. Teams are the lifeblood of any organization, driving its success and facilitating the accomplishment of its objectives. However, not all teams are created equal. The difference between a high-performing team and a mediocre one is like the difference between a symphony orchestra and a group of musicians playing their instruments out of sync. High-performance teams' function with a shared sense of purpose, clearly defined roles, open communication, and a strong culture of trust and collaboration.

The Definition of a High-Performing Team

A high-performing team can be defined as a group of people with a shared goal who collaborate effectively to achieve exceptional results. These teams are characterized by high levels of productivity, creativity, and collaboration.

Members of high-performing teams are typically highly engaged, committed to their work, and invested in the team's success. They work together efficiently, communicate effectively, and support one another to overcome challenges and achieve their objectives.

CHARACTERISTICS OF HIGH-PERFORMANCE TEAMS

A high-performing team is more than just a group of talented individuals. It is a cohesive unit that works together effectively to achieve common goals. Understanding the characteristics of high-performing teams can help leaders foster these traits within their own teams and create an environment that promotes high performance. Based on various studies and expert opinions, the following characteristics are consistently found in high-performing teams:

Building A High-Performing Team

Creating a high-performing team doesn't happen by chance; it requires careful planning, ongoing effort, and strong leadership. Building a high-performing team involves more than just bringing together a group of talented individuals. It requires fostering a culture that encourages collaboration, trust, and continuous improvement. Here are some steps that leaders can take to build a high-performing team:

Set Clear Goals: Start by defining what you want the team to achieve. Make sure these goals are SMART (Specific, Measurable, Achievable, Relevant, and Time-bound). Clearly communicate these goals to the team and ensure everyone understands their role in achieving them.

Foster Open Communication: Encourage team members to share their ideas, concerns, and feedback openly. Regular team meetings, one-on-one check-ins, and open-door policies can facilitate effective communication.

Build Trust: Trust is the foundation of high-performing teams. Leaders can foster trust by being transparent, consistent, and reliable. Encourage team members to be open and honest with each other and create a safe space where people can express their thoughts and concerns without fear of judgment or criticism.

Encourage Shared Accountability: Make sure everyone understands they are responsible for the team's success. Foster a culture where team members hold each other accountable and are committed to achieving results.

Facilitate Continuous Improvement: Encourage team members to seek feedback and look for ways to improve their performance. Provide opportunities for professional development and learning, and create an environment where mistakes are viewed as opportunities for growth.

Leverage Complementary Skills: When forming a team, consider the diverse range of skills and abilities that each member brings. Assign roles and responsibilities based on these skills to ensure the team can tackle tasks effectively.

Provide Strong Leadership: As a leader, it's your responsibility to guide the team towards its goals. This involves setting the direction, providing support and resources, motivating team members, and resolving any issues that arise.

Celebrate Success: Recognizing and celebrating the team's achievements is a powerful way to boost morale and motivation. Make sure to acknowledge individual contributions as well as team successes.

The 5 Stages of Team Development [Framework #1]

Developing a high-performing team is a gradual process that typically involves several stages. Dr. Bruce Tuckman, a psychologist and researcher, identified five stages of team development, which have become widely accepted as a useful framework for understanding team dynamics.

Forming: During the forming stage, team members are typically polite and positive, but many are also anxious and uncertain about their roles. The leader often plays a significant role in guiding the team's efforts and establishing norms.

Storming: As team members start to work together more closely, conflicts and disagreements may arise. This is the storming stage, where individuals may vie for influence, and the team may need to confront and resolve differences to move forward effectively.

Norming: In the norming stage, team members start to resolve their differences, appreciate colleagues' strengths, and respect the leader's authority. The team begins to develop a strong sense of identity and camaraderie.

Performing: The performing stage is when the team is operating as a well-organized unit. Team members are competent, autonomous, and able to handle the decision-making process without supervision. Disagreements occur but are resolved positively within the team.

Adjourning (or Mourning): This is the final stage when the team completes the task for which it was formed. The adjourning stage is characterized by a sense of achievement, and the team may celebrate the successful completion of the project.

The 5 Factors of Team Effectiveness [Framework #2]

Google's Project Aristotle identified five key dynamics that set successful teams apart. These are known as the five factors of team effectiveness:

Psychological Safety: This is the belief that one can speak their mind and take risks without fear of retribution or embarrassment. Teams with high psychological safety feel empowered to share ideas and feedback, leading to more innovative and effective problem-solving.

Dependability: On dependable teams, members reliably complete quality work on time. These builds trust within the team and ensures that all members are contributing their fair share to the team's efforts.

Structure and Clarity: High-performing teams have clear roles, plans, and goals. This allows team members to understand what is expected of them and how their work contributes to the broader objectives of the team.

Meaning: Work is personally important to team members. When team members find personal significance and satisfaction in their work, they are more motivated and engaged.

Impact: The team believes their work is purposeful and positively impacts the greater good. Knowing that the work has substantial meaning behind it can drive teams to excel.

The journey of a team through the five stages of development, while fostering the five factors of team effectiveness, increases the likelihood of achieving high performance. Leaders play a critical role in guiding their teams through these stages and cultivating these dynamics.

The 4 Key Team Performance Metrics [Framework #3]

When gauging the success of a team, it is crucial to rely on quantifiable metrics. Here are four key performance indicators that can help assess a team's effectiveness:

Productivity: This metric refers to the quantity and quality of work produced by the team within a given timeframe. It could involve tracking completed tasks, milestones reached, or overall output.

Efficiency: This measure how well the team uses its resources to achieve its goals. Efficiency might be evaluated in terms of time spent on tasks, resource utilization, or cost-effectiveness.

Cohesion: This measures the level of collaboration and cooperation within the team. Cohesion could be assessed through employee satisfaction surveys, feedback sessions, or observing the team's interactions.

Innovation: This metric evaluates the team's ability to generate and implement new ideas. It can be tracked by counting the number of new ideas implemented, improvements suggested, or patents filed, for example.

24 Key Capabilities for High-Performance Teams

Building a high-performing team is about more than just assembling a group of talented individuals. Teams also need to develop a range of capabilities that enable them to work together effectively. Here are 24 key capabilities that high-performing teams often exhibit:

Clear Communication: The ability to express ideas clearly and listen to others.

Collaboration: Working together to achieve common goals.

Conflict Resolution: Resolving disagreements in a constructive way.

Decision-Making: Making decisions in a timely and effective manner.

Delegation: Allocating tasks to the most capable individuals.

Empathy: Understanding and sharing the feelings of team members.

Feedback: Giving and receiving constructive feedback.

Flexibility: Adapting to changes and unexpected challenges.

Goal Setting: Setting clear, measurable, and achievable goals.

Innovation: Generating and implementing new ideas.

Interpersonal Skills: Building positive relationships with others.

Leadership: Guiding and inspiring others to achieve team goals.

Learning Orientation: Being open to learning and development.

Motivation: Maintaining a high level of energy and enthusiasm.

Negotiation: Reaching agreements that satisfy all parties.

Ownership: Taking responsibility for actions and outcomes.

Problem-Solving: Identifying and resolving problems effectively.

Resilience: Bouncing back from setbacks and failures.

Respect: Treating others with dignity and consideration.

Self-Awareness: Understanding one's strengths and weaknesses.

Team Building: Creating a supportive and inclusive team environment.

Trust: Building trust among team members.

Vision: Having a clear sense of direction and purpose.

Work Ethic: Demonstrating commitment, dedication, and integrity in one's work.

By focusing on developing these capabilities, teams can enhance their performance and achieve greater success.

A Framework for Developer Productivity (SPACE) [Framework #4]

The SPACE framework offers a structure for understanding and enhancing developer productivity. The acronym SPACE stands for:

Satisfaction and Well-being: For developers to be productive, they need to be satisfied with their work and maintain good physical and mental health. Factors that contribute to satisfaction include challenging work, recognition, a positive work environment, and a good work-life balance.

Performance: This refers to the developer's ability to effectively complete tasks. Performance can be influenced by the developer's skills and experience, the tools they use, and the processes in place.

Activity: This involves the actions the developer takes to complete tasks. It can include coding, debugging, collaborating with others, learning new skills, or participating in meetings.

Communication and Collaboration: Effective communication and collaboration are crucial for team-based software development. This involves sharing information, coordinating efforts, seeking help, and providing support to others.

Efficiency and Quality: This focuses on how well the developer completes tasks. Efficiency refers to the speed and resource utilization, while quality involves the correctness, usability, and reliability of the developer's work.

Why High-Performing Teams Are Critical for Business Growth

High-performing teams are integral to business growth for several reasons. They drive innovation by bringing together diverse perspectives, skills, and experiences to solve complex problems. Their high levels of productivity and efficiency lead to improved business performance and increased profitability.

By attracting and retaining top talent, these teams help build a competitive advantage for the business. They also contribute to a positive organizational culture, which can enhance employee engagement, customer satisfaction, and brand reputation.

The Secret to Keeping High-Performers Engaged

High performers are critical assets for any organization but keeping them engaged requires thoughtful effort. Here are a few strategies:

Challenge them: High performers thrive on challenging tasks and opportunities to learn and grow. Providing them with complex projects and continuous learning opportunities can help maintain their engagement.

Recognize their contributions: High performers want their efforts to be acknowledged. Regular feedback and recognition can help them feel valued and motivated.

Offer autonomy: High performers are often self-motivated and value the ability to work independently. Giving them autonomy over their work can increase their job satisfaction and engagement.

Provide opportunities for advancement: High performers are typically ambitious and look for opportunities to advance their careers. Clear career paths and opportunities for progression can help keep them engaged and committed to the organization.

ADDRESSING COMMON TEAM CHALLENGES

Effective leadership requires the ability to identify and overcome challenges that can prevent teams from reaching their full potential. While each team is unique and may face different obstacles, certain challenges are common across industries and organizations. These can include issues related to communication, conflict, motivation, performance, and cohesion. Leaders can address these challenges by promoting open communication, providing feedback and recognition, fostering trust and collaboration, and making a concerted effort to address issues promptly and effectively. This section provides a comprehensive exploration of common team challenges and strategies to overcome them.

Understanding Team Challenges

Before solutions can be proposed and applied, understanding the common challenges teams face is a crucial first step. These challenges can include ineffective communication, lack of trust, conflict and disagreements, lack of clear goals, and differences in work styles and personalities.

Strategies for Effective Communication

Open, transparent, and respectful communication forms the bedrock of high-performing teams. Techniques for improving communication may include regular team meetings, training on effective communication practices, use of collaborative tools, and promoting a culture where feedback is welcomed.

Building Trust within Teams

Trust is integral for the smooth functioning of a team. Strategies for building trust can involve creating a safe space where team members feel comfortable sharing their thoughts, celebrating team successes, and promoting behaviors that demonstrate reliability, consistency, and honesty.

Managing and Resolving Conflict

Disagreements and conflicts are inevitable in any team setting. The key is to ensure that these are managed and resolved in a constructive manner. Techniques can include conflict resolution training, mediation, fostering an environment where differing viewpoints are respected, and encouraging open dialogue.

Motivating Teams

Keeping a team motivated can be a significant challenge, especially during demanding projects. Strategies for maintaining motivation include regular recognition of team members' efforts, providing opportunities for professional development, and ensuring that workloads are balanced and fair.

Enhancing Team Performance

Team performance can be improved by clearly defining roles and responsibilities, setting measurable goals, providing constructive feedback, and offering the necessary resources and support for team members to excel at their tasks.

Fostering Team Cohesion

A cohesive team is greater than the sum of its individual members. Building team cohesion can be achieved through team-building activities, creating a shared vision and goals, promoting mutual respect and understanding, and encouraging collaboration and mutual support.

Handling Diversity in Teams

Teams often consist of individuals with different backgrounds, skills, experiences, and perspectives. While this diversity can be a strength, it can also lead to misunderstandings and conflicts. Strategies for handling diversity include diversity and inclusion training, promoting a culture of respect and acceptance, and leveraging the unique skills and perspectives of each team member.

In addressing these challenges, the role of the leader is crucial. By fostering a supportive, inclusive, and collaborative team environment, leaders can help their teams navigate these challenges and achieve high performance.

Practical Tips and Strategies for Addressing Team Challenges

To create and sustain high-performance in teams, managers need to adopt effective strategies to tackle the challenges they face. Here are some practical tips:

Enhancing Communication

Use appropriate communication tools: Choose the communication tools that best fit your team's needs.

This could range from emails, video conferencing tools, to project management software.

Hold regular meetings: Schedule weekly or bi-weekly meetings to keep everyone in the loop and address any issues promptly.

Encourage feedback: Foster an environment where team members feel comfortable sharing their thoughts and ideas. You could have a suggestion box or anonymous feedback system.

Boosting Motivation

Recognize effort: Acknowledge the efforts of your team members regularly. This could be in team meetings, through emails or even on a public platform.

Provide opportunities for growth: Offer opportunities for skill development or advancement to team members. This could be in the form of workshops, trainings or mentoring.

Create a positive work environment: Ensure the workplace is conducive for productivity. This includes making sure that team members have all the resources they need and treating everyone with respect and fairness.

Resolving Conflicts

Encourage open dialogue: Promote a culture where team members feel safe to express their feelings and views. This can be achieved through regular team discussions and creating an environment that values differing opinions.

Mediate effectively: If conflicts arise, intervene in a fair and neutral way. Understand the root cause of the conflict, and help the parties involved come to a resolution.

Increasing Productivity

Clearly define roles: Ensure that everyone in the team knows their responsibilities. This could be done through detailed job descriptions or during team meetings.

Set realistic goals: Use the SMART (Specific, Measurable, Achievable, Relevant, Time-bound) framework for setting team goals.

Provide resources and support: Make sure your team has all the necessary tools and resources to do their jobs effectively. This could include providing access to relevant software, proper training, and support for their physical and mental well-being.

By using these strategies, managers can effectively address team challenges, promote positive team dynamics, and create a high-performing team.

Six Common Team Challenges – How to Overcome Them and Grow Your Team

Drawing from the resources, here are six common challenges that teams often encounter, with solutions to overcome them:

Unclear Goals and Direction: This can lead to confusion and frustration among team members. To counter this, ensure goals are clearly communicated, understood, and aligned with the company's objectives.

Poor Communication: This can lead to misunderstandings, reduced productivity, and low morale. Foster open and clear communication by implementing effective communication tools and encouraging feedback.

Conflict and Trust Issues: These can lead to a toxic work environment. Encourage a culture of respect, promote open dialogue for conflict resolution, and foster trust-building activities.

Lack of Engagement: This can lead to reduced productivity and high turnover rates. Boost engagement by recognizing effort, providing opportunities for growth, and creating a positive work environment.

Role Ambiguity: This can cause confusion and result in tasks being overlooked. Ensure roles and responsibilities are clearly defined and understood by everyone.

Resistance to Change: This can hinder growth and innovation. Foster a culture that embraces change, provide training and support during transitions, and communicate the benefits and reasons for the change clearly.

TEAM-BUILDING ACTIVITIES THAT WORK

Building a high-performance team involves more than just professional development. It also requires creating a positive team culture where everyone feels valued and understood. Team-building activities can play a crucial role in this process by improving team dynamics, fostering better communication, and building trust among team members. They offer a fun and engaging way for team members to connect, collaborate, and understand each other better. This, in turn, can lead to better collaboration, improved morale, and higher productivity.

The Benefits of Team-Building Activities

Team-building activities offer a host of benefits for teams and organizations as a whole. Some of these benefits include improved communication, increased collaboration, better problem-solving abilities, and improved interpersonal relationships.

Moreover, team-building activities can help in identifying and leveraging individual strengths, which can further contribute to team success. They provide a safe and enjoyable environment for team members to develop and strengthen their skills, fostering a culture of continuous learning and improvement.

Indoor and Outdoor Team-Building Activities

There are numerous team-building activities that organizations can employ, each designed to meet specific objectives. For instance, problem-solving activities can improve critical thinking and decision-making skills, while communication activities can help foster better understanding and cooperation among team members. On the other hand, trust-building activities can help in building a supportive and trusting team environment.

For indoor activities, consider games such as 'Escape Rooms' where team members must work together to solve puzzles and escape from a locked room. This activity promotes communication, collaboration, and problem-solving. Similarly, 'Building Bridges' requires teams to construct a bridge using provided materials, promoting creativity and teamwork.

For outdoor activities, 'Treasure Hunts' or 'Scavenger Hunts' can be organized, where teams compete to find a list of items or complete a series of tasks. These activities foster teamwork, communication, and strategic thinking.

Virtual Team-Building Activities

With the rise of remote work, virtual team-building activities have gained popularity. These activities are designed to engage remote teams and foster a sense of connection and camaraderie among team members, despite the physical distance. Activities such as virtual quizzes, online game competitions, and virtual coffee breaks can help in keeping remote teams engaged and connected.

Tailoring Team-Building Activities to Your Team's Needs

While there are many team-building activities to choose from, it's important to tailor them to your team's specific needs and characteristics. Consider your team's size, diversity, preferences, and the specific challenges they're facing. For instance, if your team is struggling with communication, activities that promote open and effective communication would be beneficial.

Remember, the goal of these activities is not just to have fun, but to build a stronger, more cohesive team. So, always debrief after each activity to reflect on the learnings and how they can be applied in the team's day-to-day work.

Specific Team-Building Activities and Exercises

Team-building activities need to cater to all levels and personalities within the team to ensure maximum engagement and effectiveness. These activities should not only foster collaboration and improve communication but also cater to different interests and skills to ensure everyone on the team feels included and valued. Here are some specific exercises that can be effective for various personalities and levels within the team:

Icebreakers: These are short activities used to introduce team members to each other and encourage open communication. An example of an icebreaker activity could be "Two Truths and a Lie," where each member shares two truths and one lie about themselves, and others have to guess the lie.

Problem-Solving Exercises: These exercises can improve critical thinking and collaboration. For example, "The Egg Drop Challenge" requires teams to design a contraption using limited materials to prevent an egg from breaking when dropped from a certain height.

Trust-Building Activities: These exercises aim to build trust among team members. The "Blindfold Obstacle Course" exercise is one example where one team member guides a blindfolded teammate through an obstacle course, fostering trust and communication.

Communication Exercises: These activities are designed to enhance communication within the team. For example, "Back-to-Back Drawing" requires pairs to sit back-to-back with one person describing a picture and the other trying to draw it based only on the description.

Collaboration Exercises: These activities help team members to work together more effectively. A popular example is "The Human Knot," where team members must untangle themselves without breaking hand connections, promoting cooperation and teamwork.

Outdoor Adventure Games: For teams that enjoy physical activity, outdoor games can be a great option. Activities like "Capture the Flag," "Relay Races," or even "Team Sports" like soccer or baseball can foster team spirit and cooperation.

Remember, the success of these activities lies in their ability to cater to the diverse needs and preferences of your team while also addressing key areas for improvement. After each exercise, take time to debrief and discuss the lessons learned, ensuring the skills developed during the activities are transferred to the workplace.

Examples of Effective Team-Building Activities

Here are some team-building activities that can foster collaboration and mutual respect among team members:

Scavenger Hunts: This activity is a fun and engaging way to encourage teamwork and problem-solving skills. Team members must work together to find items or complete tasks based on a set of clues.

Escape Rooms: These provide a unique challenge that requires collaboration, creative thinking, and effective communication. Teams must work together to solve puzzles and riddles to escape from a locked room within a certain time limit.

Building Challenges: Exercises such as building a tower with limited materials can stimulate creativity and encourage teams to cooperate and think strategically.

Trust Exercises: These activities can help build trust and rapport among team members. An example is the classic "trust fall," where one person falls backward, relying on their teammates to catch them.

Personality Tests and Discussions: This activity can help team members better understand each other's work styles, strengths, and weaknesses, promoting empathy and effective collaboration.

Cooking Challenges: Similar to popular TV shows, these can encourage teamwork, creativity, and time management skills, as teams work together to prepare a meal under a time constraint.

Story:

Drawing upon real-life stories can indeed provide valuable insights into how to instill passion into a team and create successful work environments. Here are two compelling stories drawn from these threads:

Story 1: The Power of Autonomy and Trust

A Reddit user who goes by the handle archaic_thing describes their experience in a successful team:

"The most successful team I've been a part of was an independent unit within a larger organization. We were given a high degree of autonomy, which allowed us to develop and maintain our own unique culture. We had a high level of trust within the team, and everyone was committed to helping each other succeed. We had clearly defined roles and responsibilities, but we also had the freedom to contribute outside of our designated areas. Our leadership was supportive and hands-off, giving us the space to innovate and solve problems in our own way. It was the kind of environment where everyone felt valued and empowered, and this passion translated into high-quality work and high levels of satisfaction."

Story 2: The Importance of Shared Vision and Mutual Respect

Another Reddit user, abey_m, shares an inspiring story about transforming a demotivated team:

"I took over a team that was demotivated and lacked passion due to constant changes in leadership and vision. The first thing I did was to listen to their concerns and understand their perspectives. I acknowledged their frustrations and made it clear that their voices mattered.

We then worked together to establish a clear vision and goals for the team. This gave everyone a sense of purpose and direction. I also made an effort to build personal relationships with each team member and foster a culture of respect and mutual support. We started celebrating small wins and appreciating each other's contributions. Over time, the team became more engaged and passionate about their work. They started collaborating more effectively and produced higher quality work.

The transformation didn't happen overnight, and it required a lot of patience and persistence. But seeing the team come together and become more passionate about their work was one of the most rewarding experiences of my career."

Both stories demonstrate how effective leadership, defined by trust, autonomy, shared vision, and mutual respect, can foster a passionate and successful team. These stories underscore the reality that the team's success is inherently connected to the quality of leadership and the environment that nurtures its growth.

Chapter Summary and Key Takeaways:

In this chapter, we delved deep into the concept of team-building activities, emphasizing their role in enhancing team dynamics, boosting communication, and building trust. We established that team building is an essential process that boosts team cohesion, improves productivity, and enhances interpersonal relationships within a group.

We discussed a wide array of team-building activities, including ice breakers, problem-solving tasks, trust-building exercises, and team celebrations. These activities, when implemented thoughtfully and systematically, can significantly bolster team morale and productivity. We also recognized the importance of customizing activities to address specific team goals and challenges, thus ensuring that every exercise is purposeful and directly beneficial to the team's development.

The chapter also incorporated compelling stories from experienced leaders who effectively instilled passion in their teams. These narratives demonstrated the importance of trust, shared vision, mutual respect, and individual empowerment in creating a passionate, committed team.

In the next chapter, titled 'Mastering Leadership Communication,' we will delve into the intricate dynamics of communication within leadership. This includes understanding the importance of communication skills, exploring different communication styles, and offering practical tips and strategies for improving your communication as a leader.

As we transition into this next section, we invite you to reflect on your communication style and how it impacts your team. Just as we explored in this chapter, great leadership is a journey of continuous learning and adaptation. As we begin the next phase of that journey, let's strive to make our communication as effective and impactful as possible.

CHAPTER 4
MASTERING LEADERSHIP COMMUNICATION

> *"To effectively communicate, we must realize that we are all different in how we perceive the world and use this understanding to guide our communication with others."*
>
> TONY ROBBINS, AUTHOR, SPEAKER, COACH

Communication is essential for effective leadership because it is central to building and fostering relationships within a team, fostering creativity and innovation, and effectively motivating team members. Leaders must effectively convey their vision, goals, and expectations to their team members to inspire and motivate them. Additionally, leaders must be able to listen actively to their team members, understand their concerns and feedback, and provide clear and concise guidance.

While many different skills are involved in effective leadership, communication is one of the most important. Imagine a hypothetical scenario where a leader has power and authority but lacks communication skills. Such a leader would likely have difficulty building trust and rapport with their team members, ensuring their work is aligned with organizational goals, and motivating the team to achieve the desired results.

Communication is central to effective leadership because it builds relationships between leaders and their followers, ensures that both work towards shared goals, and motivates followers to achieve them. In other words, effective leadership requires excellent communication skills.

UNDERSTANDING EFFECTIVE LEADERSHIP COMMUNICATION?

Leadership communication is the process leaders use to communicate their vision, goals, and expectations to their team members. Leaders must effectively convey their ideas and message and inspire positive action from team members.

Effective leadership communication involves four key components: clarity, inspiration, alignment with organizational goals, and commitment level. These are discussed in detail below:

Clarity refers to how a message is conveyed to followers. A leader's messages should be easy for team members to understand without requiring much explanation or interpretation. If a leader's messages are ambiguous or confusing, they could lead to confusion and disagreement between the leaders and their followers. Additionally, leaders must be honest, genuine, and authentic in communicating with team members. If a leader tries to deceive or manipulate their team members through false messages, they will lose their trust and respect. Indeed, research has found that public figures who use deceptive communication tactics tend to be less effective at influencing people than those who communicate authentically (Agnew & Ugrinowitch, 2010).

Inspiration refers to how leaders motivate their followers through their communication. Effective communication inspires team members to take specific action for a specific purpose. The goal is for team members to be inspired to have that "A-ha!" moment and realize that the mission is worthwhile and unique. This, in turn, will increase their commitment level towards the mission.

Alignment with organizational goals refers to how effective leaders communicate their messages so that they are by the overall organizational goals. For example, suppose a leader has recently been promoted and thus feels pressure to perform well. In that case, they may bring this stress into their communication with others because it will likely influence their performance (Cronbach & Meehl, 1955). As a result, they may be more negative and critical in their communication, which could undermine the team's ability to perform well (Locke & Latham, 2002).

Commitment level refers to how committed team members are to the goals of their leaders. If team members are not motivated or invested in achieving these goals, then they will likely be less successful at achieving these goals. Effective leadership communication inspires followers to commit to their leader's vision. This will increase team members' motivation to achieve their leader's goals. Effective communication motivates us to act per our self-interest and having a sense of commitment toward a leader can be an important source of motivation.

Effective communication is important for leaders because it helps them shape how their followers think and act. While communication over the Internet has become more prevalent in recent years, face-to-face conversations remain crucial for effective leadership.

Leaders who cannot communicate face-to-face effectively are likely unable to maintain good relationships and support within their team and may also be less effective at communicating with others across geographical distances.

What Are the Best Practices for Effective Leadership Communication?

How effective leaders use their communication skills to inspire team members to achieve their goals is a function of three things: the leader's ability to effectively communicate their message, the type of team members who are in the leader's environment, and the level of trust that exists between leaders and followers. These factors are discussed below:

Leaders can use five communication practices to encourage open communication: encouraging questions and suggestions, maintaining timely updates, providing examples and vivid details, sharing relevant information with followers, and accepting that not all ideas will be good.

Encouraging questions and suggestions: Leaders should encourage their followers to voice concerns, ideas, questions, or suggestions. For example, suppose a follower asks his manager a question about an assignment or project he is working on. In that case, the manager should actively listen instead of immediately attempting to solve the problem for the employee. The manager should then ask follow-up questions to clarify the individual's concerns, ideas, questions, or suggestions. In this way, the manager ensures that they have a full understanding of the issue being raised.

Maintaining timely updates: Good leaders should provide regular updates to their team members to ensure everyone is on the same page and aligned with organizational goals. Providing timely updates encourages team members to actively participate in discussions because they can contribute their thoughts and suggestions about issues when they arise. However, it is important for leaders not to overload team members with too many details about organizational issues because this could overwhelm them and cause confusion or anxiety.

Providing examples and vivid details: Leaders should give followers enough information to help them understand the reasoning behind their decisions or actions. For example, if a leader wants his team to work more efficiently, he can illustrate this point by providing a specific example of how he thinks the team could do this better. In this way, followers can understand how they can be more effective in their jobs and contribute to the organization's mission.

Sharing relevant information with followers: Constantly updated communication does not necessarily result in effective leadership communication. For instance, some leaders provide so much information about their goals and expectations that team members become confused. It is, therefore, important for leaders to be clear about what they expect from their team members.

Asking open-ended questions about followers' opinions and needs will help leaders identify the best ways to motivate and encourage them to participate in the organization's mission actively. It is also important for leaders to respond candidly when team members provide input or suggestions, even if these ideas are not what the leader initially expected or wanted.

Accepting that not all ideas will be good: Leaders should expect their team members to have different opinions, but they must accept that their followers can still contribute good ideas that may benefit the organization. For example, if a follower suggests that the leader can improve their leadership role by being more approachable, it does not mean they are challenging the leadership role. Just because the leader may not have thought this way doesn't mean they should reject this idea as worthless. At the same time, leaders should recognize that there are many good ideas that they cannot immediately accept. Good ideas regarding organizational goals and resources must be evaluated before being implemented successfully.

What Are the Barriers to Effective Leadership Communication?

Effective leadership communication is difficult because leaders must communicate with their team members and followers in a way that encourages them to understand the leader's message fully but does not overwhelm them to the point of becoming frustrated.

Barriers to effective communication include language barriers, lack of mutual trust, management styles, organizational culture and values, and communication channels. Leaders who cannot communicate face-to-face with their employees effectively will have difficulty achieving meaningful teamwork across geographical distances.

Language barriers: Leaders must be able to communicate their messages in various languages effectively.

Silence: Effective communication also requires leaders not to engage in "silent treatment," where followers are not allowed to respond.

Lack of mutual trust: Effective leadership communication is unlikely if team members do not trust their leader or if the leader does not trust their followers. For example, leaders should give their team members adequate opportunities to confront them about issues rather than trying to solve problems for them before they can voice their concerns. Leaders should also provide team members with the relevant information needed to make informed decisions rather than telling them what to do.

Differing management styles: Differences in leadership styles can cause difficulties in effective communication. Each style has its advantages, as well as its disadvantages. For example, a me-oriented style would not be appropriate for a situation where team members are expected to meet or communicate with each other on an ongoing basis which may result in mistrust and disagreements.

Differences in organizational culture and values: Effective communication relies upon each individual's perception of appropriate behavior; however, cultural differences can cause misunderstanding. Additionally, different approaches to leadership may lead to different levels of acceptance from followers because followers may still have different expectations about acceptable behaviors.

Differences in communication channels: Specific communication channels vary depending on the type of organization and the relationship between leader and follower. For example, in a work-oriented organization, followers may have more opportunities for informal communication between team members; however, leaders can have lower expectations if they expect their followers to provide formal reports.

Common Leadership Communication Problems you may face (And How to Correct Them)

The following are some common problems that leaders often encounter during communication and how to correct them.

1. Lack of proper attitude: You should not avoid talking with your team members if there is a problem. Issues can be more easily resolved if they are dealt with early on in a non-threatening manner. Seek to understand the problem and why it exists before attempting to resolve it.

2. Lacking good time management skills: With so many responsibilities as leaders, we might not be able to communicate with the team members as often as we would like to. You should take a proactive approach and set up regular meetings during which you can discuss issues with the team members. It might be beneficial to schedule the meetings when other team members can attend.

3. **Not listening to others:** Sometimes, we listen rather than try to understand what others say. Avoid doing this as much as possible when communicating with your team members. Try taking notes when someone is speaking. This will help you remember their comments accurately.

4. Not giving feedback: You should give positive feedback on good behavior to encourage others to keep up their good work and avoid negative behavior in the future. Negative feedback should be meted out in a constructive manner, not in an intimidating one.

5. **Not involving team members in the decision-making process:** You should let your teammates participate as much as possible in the decision-making process. This will encourage them to feel more involved and committed to the team's goals.

6. **Failing to acknowledge success:** You should always praise good work, especially when it is done by a teammate who previously has been performing below expectations. Acknowledging successes will help motivate your team members to keep up their good work while avoiding pitfalls and mistakes will result in higher productivity levels within your team/company/business.

7. Failing to understand your team's communication style: Team members usually do not want their leader to use the same communication style as them. However, you should be aware of your teammates' preferred communication styles and try to accommodate them accordingly.

8. Being impatient: You should avoid being impatient when communicating with your team members, no matter how important the message is that you want to deliver. Being patient will force you to listen attentively, and doing so will certainly make others feel more comfortable about communicating with you in the future.

While many different models for effective leadership communication exist, many of the same key elements are prevalent. Through a variety of different styles and methods, effective leaders must be able to:

The following are the three most important guidelines for effective communication.

1. Closed-loop communications - closed-loop communication is "communication that includes information to and from each person repeatedly during an interactional episode. It includes at least one person talking about and with another person."

2. Feedback is "information communicated from one actor to another to allow them to modify their behavior."

3. Informative speech is "a communication act which involves the direct and informative expression of a speaker's thoughts or feelings through factual information, opinions, advice, or prescriptions."

For any leader to successfully communicate effectively with their team members and followers, knowing what is expected of them will make communication much easier.

THE ART OF GIVING FEEDBACK

Understand the Different Types of Feedback

Many different types of feedback are often seen in the workplace. You need to understand which type of feedback your team members prefer, as it can help to communicate the type of feedback, they are most comfortable receiving.

Types of feedback include:

1. Positive Feedback: Positive feedback is used to acknowledge and reinforce desirable behaviors, accomplishments, or strengths of an individual or team member. It focuses on recognizing achievements, encouraging continued performance, and boosting morale. Positive feedback helps to create a supportive and motivating work environment where employees feel valued and appreciated for their contributions.

2. Constructive Feedback: Constructive feedback aims to identify areas for improvement or suggest changes to behaviors, processes, or outcomes. It is crucial for development and growth, highlighting areas where individuals or teams can enhance performance. Constructive feedback should be specific, actionable, and focused on behaviors rather than personal traits. It is important to deliver constructive feedback in a respectful and supportive manner to encourage learning and development.

3. Motivational Feedback: Motivational feedback inspires and energizes individuals or teams to enhance performance. It focuses on highlighting individuals' potential, strengths, and growth opportunities. Motivational feedback can be particularly effective in boosting confidence, encouraging creativity, and fostering a sense of ownership and commitment to achieving goals.

4. Corrective Feedback: Corrective feedback is provided when there is a need to address performance issues or correct inappropriate behaviors. Delivering corrective feedback promptly and directly is essential, focusing on specific actions or behaviors that need improvement. Constructive criticism and clear expectations can help individuals understand what needs to be changed and how to enhance their performance.

5. Continuous Feedback: Continuous feedback is an ongoing process that involves regular communication and coaching between leaders and team members. It provides timely guidance, support, and recognition, promoting a culture of continuous learning and improvement. Continuous feedback allows for immediate course correction, alignment of expectations, and the developing of stronger working relationships.

6. Impact feedback: Impact feedback is provided to evaluate the effects of decision-making and actions on strategic goals. It focuses on the next steps after an action or outcome, allowing individuals and teams to assess the impact of their decisions. Impact feedback helps identify key learnings, areas for improvement, and opportunities for future actions.

7. Feedback Styles: There are four different styles of feedback in a workplace, including 360-degree feedback, opportunity feedback, need-based feedback, and catastrophic feedback. 360-degree feedback is used to gather input about an individual's performance from multiple sources in the workplace. It can be particularly useful in identifying strengths and development areas to help leaders deliver effective performance evaluations or design developmental plans with individual team members.

Why Impact Feedback Is the Most Effective Type of Feedback

Impact feedback is the most effective type as it is specific, timely, and focused on results. It is the most direct and immediate way to provide clear, specific feedback to individuals or teams, encouraging them to focus on the tasks. By providing detailed feedback about performance and progress, leaders help team members recognize areas for improvement and growth, enabling them to make informed decisions on how best to achieve goals.

When the effects of impact feedback are positive or constructive, leaders can use it for continuous improvement. Reviewing results from previous events and action steps taken by the individual or team member can highlight improvement areas. Leaders can also use impact feedback to identify gaps between expectations and desired results for different areas of responsibility. Additionally, leaders can use impact feedback to evaluate the impact of their decisions and actions on achieving key goals.

Avoid These 10 Common Mistakes in Giving Feedback

According to experts, leaders make some common mistakes when giving feedback.

1. Taking feedback personally: Strive to develop a thick skin to handle constructive criticism and feedback. Leaders need to make data-driven decisions and receive honest feedback without taking it personally. Leaders should acknowledge the importance of constructive criticism by seeking honest and accurate feedback from several sources.

2. Making assumptions: Leaders often assume that their team understands what they want or need without clearly communicating the desired outcome or impact of a decision or action. For example, a leader may assume that the team is aware of new procedures or policies without communicating them clearly to the team in advance.

3. Allowing toxic feedback: Avoid all forms of toxic feedback because it can lead to defensiveness, low team morale, and counterproductive behavior. Leaders must be sensitive to the emotions and feelings of individuals within their team. They should also provide guidance and coaching in times of stress.

4. Not providing follow-up: It is important to provide feedback as quickly as possible so that recipients can adjust or incorporate it into routine work activities more effectively. For example, a leader may have concerns about an individual's performance or capabilities but may not have time for a follow-up meeting for another two weeks.

5. Inappropriate feedback: Leaders should avoid providing negative, disparaging, or discriminatory feedback because it can cause emotional distress and damage the trust levels between them and the individual.

6. Giving feedback after the meeting: Providing timely feedback in person is important to prevent leaders from giving their team members incorrect information or putting them on the spot for a quick decision. For example, a leader may meet with an employee to address his performance reviews for over 2 hours each month to provide timely feedback. But by doing so, it may be difficult for employees to focus on their responsibilities during this extended conversation when so many other distractions are present.

7. Blaming the individual: It is important to avoid blaming the individual by focusing on the facts and providing constructive feedback. Suggesting something "wrong" with a person or a team is toxic because it can lead to defensiveness, low team morale, and counterproductive behavior.

8. **Overgeneralizing:** Focus on the specific details of each situation to avoid overgeneralizing and making broad generalizations. It is also important to consider the individual's overall environment and the performance review context.

Avoiding feedback mistakes

There are several key factors to consider customizing the feedback and avoid resistance:

Behaviors versus Traits: Focusing on specific behaviors rather than personal traits is crucial when giving feedback. Behaviors are observable and can be modified, while traits are inherent characteristics that are difficult to change. Addressing behaviors makes the feedback more actionable and helps individuals understand what they can do differently.

Modality Matters: The way feedback is delivered can significantly impact its effectiveness and reception. Different individuals may respond better to certain feedback modalities, such as face-to-face discussions, written feedback, or group settings. Understanding the preferences and communication styles of the recipients can help tailor the feedback approach for better engagement and receptiveness.

Timing: Timely feedback is essential to make it relevant and impactful. Feedback should be provided as close to the observed behavior or event as possible. Waiting too long may diminish the recipient's ability to connect the feedback with the specific situation, reducing its effectiveness. However, it's important to strike a balance and not rush to provide feedback, allowing both parties to reflect and approach the discussion with a level head.

Follow-Up: Following up on previous feedback discussions is a crucial step in the feedback process. It demonstrates commitment and shows that the feedback was taken seriously. Follow-up conversations allow progress monitoring, clarifications, and further guidance if needed. They also provide an opportunity to acknowledge and reinforce positive changes or address lingering concerns.

How to Give Effective Feedback

There are many ways to communicate feedback effectively and lead to better results. Here are some tips:

Be specific: Give examples and provide specifics so the recipient knows exactly what they did.

Be timely: Feedback should be given at the right time, on the same topic, or in response to ongoing or recent behavior. Timing is essential to provide effective feedback because it helps recipients connect your feedback with past events and current situations. A good trick for keeping track of when comments would have been most helpful is to put a note in a calendar "in case" you have an upcoming meeting or conversation about an issue you know will come up again soon.

Be open: Listen to the other person's point of view. Openness also allows for feedback to be provided without emotional overreaction or hostility.

Consider others: Remember that various people are involved in a situation, and it is important to consider their feelings, actions, and motivations.

Benefits of Feedback in the Workplace

Feedback is a positive process that can have many benefits — for the person giving feedback, the person receiving it, and the organization.

1. Recognition

Providing an honest appraisal of your employee's performance is often considered one of the most difficult parts of being a manager. Yet it can be equally valuable to them and helpful to you in developing their skills. The right kind of feedback lets your employees know you care about their well-being, want them to grow professionally and personally, and will help them improve their job performance.

2. Validation

Valuing your employees as a person is crucial to their personal growth and your ability to offer them the mentoring guidance and other support, they need to reach their maximum potential. Giving negative feedback lets them better understand why you are dissatisfied with them and find solutions for future failure rather than dwelling on it.

Feedback can also help employees understand what's expected of them. By discussing performance, both parties learn how to perform better when the circumstances arise again. This is particularly important for new employees who may not know how things should be done at their company.

3. Personal Growth

Although it can be difficult for some to accept negative feedback, it will help them grow personally in the long run. The goal is to look beyond inaccurate self-assessments, take responsibility for their actions, and correct them instead of blaming others or manipulating the situation.

4. Learning Opportunities

Once you have identified the employee's deficiency, offer suggestions on how they can improve in the future. This keeps employees accountable and allows you to show your mentoring skills by helping them understand how they can do better. It also helps with future performance evaluation.

ENCOURAGING EFFECTIVE FUTURE BEHAVIOR

Encouraging effective future behavior among employees is crucial for maintaining a motivated and high-performing team. Here are strategies and tips on how managers can achieve this:

Setting Clear Goals: Clearly defining goals provides employees with a sense of direction and purpose. When setting goals, make sure they are specific, measurable, attainable, relevant, and time-bound (SMART goals).

Providing Regular Feedback: Regular feedback is essential for employee growth and improvement. Offer constructive feedback promptly, focusing on both strengths and areas for improvement.

Offering Incentives: Incentives can be powerful motivators for employees. They can be financial rewards, bonuses, or non-monetary benefits—tailor incentives to align with the interests and preferences of your team members.

Recognizing Achievements: Recognizing and celebrating employees' achievements boosts morale and motivation. Acknowledge their accomplishments publicly within the team or organization wide. Offer personalized recognition, such as verbal appreciation, handwritten notes, or public praise.

Providing Opportunities for Growth and Development: Employees value opportunities for growth and development. Offer training programs, workshops, or conferences to enhance their skills and knowledge.

Foster a Positive Work Environment: Create a positive work environment that promotes teamwork, open communication, and collaboration. Encourage a healthy work-life balance and show genuine concern for employee well-being.

Lead by Example: Managers play a vital role in motivating employees. Lead by example and demonstrate the behavior you expect from your team. Show enthusiasm, commitment, and a strong work ethic.

8 Ways to Get the Employee Behavior You Want:

- Communicate clearly what you want them to change.
- Discuss actions they can take to improve.
- Identify the behaviors you want, not the ones you don't.
- Provide positive reinforcement when they get it right.
- Define the time frame for improvement.
- Set up a follow-up meeting, and act on what was discussed.
- Test for new behaviors before praising performance for those changes.
- Recognize that some improvements may be slow and difficult, so be patient and don't give up too easily.

Scientifically Proven Ways to Motivate Employees

One of the most common workplace complaints is that employees don't feel motivated. A recent Gallup poll found only 38 percent of American workers are "thriving" at work. So, what do we have to do to get employees motivated?

At its core, motivation is about satisfying physical needs like food or shelter or psychological needs like autonomy and relatedness. In the workplace, there are eight scientifically proven ways to motivate employees:

1. Fairness: People enjoy working for fair managers who treat everyone equally and consistently apply the rules and standards equitably.

2. Positive Goals: People like working for a supportive manager who encourages them to be their best, which can be accomplished through clear, realistic performance goals.

3. Autonomy: People like working for a manager who gives them the room and freedom to do their jobs well and feel good about themselves.

4. Commitment: People want managers they know they can count on, meaning they need managers with whom they can commit to building a long-lasting relationship of trust and respect. (You can't say you care about your employees if you don't know how much and how often you communicate with them.)

5. Partnership: People like working in a team where they can be themselves and make a real difference.

6. Learning: People often say they have a passion for learning and growing, so it's important to provide avenues for their learning. (Providing learning opportunities through training, conferences, or meetings that provide content and support may be more effective.)

7. Interdependence: People like working with people who are like them and are willing to work on the same goals with them, as well as develop common ground—for example, when you get married, you decide whether you want to live in an apartment or house or city; independent companies may want to consider doing this as well.

8. Connection: People like working with people they can trust and value, so it's important to create an atmosphere of mutual trust, respect, and feelings of connection. For example, positive relationships at the workplace can be characterized by observing a 'we-feeling' rather than an 'I-feeling' between employees.

Chapter Summary and Key Takeaways:

Chapter 4 took us on a journey through the realm of leadership communication. We recognized that the ability to communicate effectively is a pivotal skill in successful leadership. We addressed common communication challenges that leaders often face and offered strategies to surmount these hurdles. In particular, we emphasized the importance of active listening, clear messaging, and empathetic communication in fostering a productive dialogue with team members.

Furthermore, we delved into the art of giving feedback, discussing its role in maintaining a high-performing team. We explored different types of feedback and discussed strategies for their effective delivery. Emphasizing the need for feedback to be specific, timely, and balanced, we also offered insight into creating a culture of feedback within a team.

We also tackled the task of encouraging effective future behavior among team members. We shared evidence-based strategies for motivating employees, including setting clear goals, providing regular feedback, recognizing achievements, and fostering opportunities for growth and development.

The chapter concluded with inspiring stories highlighting the role of good communication in fostering a healthy relationship with leaders. These narratives showed how open dialogue and effective feedback can boost team morale and performance.

As we step into the next chapter, 'Empowering Your Team through Coaching and Delegation,' we will explore ways to further uplift your team, enabling them to reach new heights of performance. In this chapter, we will discover how coaching, and delegation are key tools that successful leaders use to empower their teams. They provide opportunities for team members to develop their skills, take on more responsibilities, and grow both personally and professionally. As we journey onward, let's remember that effective leadership is about empowering others to achieve their best.

INSPIRING OTHER LEADERS

> *"To command is to serve, nothing more and nothing less."*
>
> ANDRE MALRAUX

A mark of a great leader is their drive to help others succeed. That might be their team members, their peers, or a friend at a different company. With every facet of the leadership skill set you're nurturing, this drive inside you is growing, and you'll be taking every opportunity to help your staff grow and develop.

But your skills don't just turn off when you leave the office – you'll carry everything forward into every area of life, and that's only going to be a good thing for those around you.

Even at this stage, you can help out other leaders as they navigate their developmental path – regardless of whether you ever meet them face to face… and the even better news is that it barely has to make a dent in your busy schedule.

All it takes is a short review of this book, and you'll help other people who want to develop their skills as a leader to find the guidance they're looking for – just as you will for your team as you strive to push them forward to the next step on their career path.

By leaving a review of this book on Amazon, you'll show other managers the doorway to the guidance they're looking for.

Simply by telling new readers how this book has helped you and what they'll find inside it, you'll point them in the direction of the advice they need to uplevel their skills and become the successful leader they long to be.

I'm truly grateful for your support in helping others succeed… and that's a sure sign of an excellent leader.

CHAPTER 5
EMPOWERING YOUR TEAM THROUGH COACHING AND DELEGATION

> "People want guidance, not rhetoric. They need to know the action plan and how it will be implemented. They want to be given the responsibility to help solve the problem and authority to act on it."
>
> HOWARD SCHULTZ, POUR YOUR HEART INTO IT: HOW STARBUCKS BUILT A COMPANY ONE CUP AT A TIME

THE MANAGER TOOLS DELEGATION MODEL

The Manager Tools Delegation Model is an eight-step framework that will help you build a habit of effective delegation and ensure the progress of your projects. You can use it to delegate any project, whether you are the manager or want to help the person who reports to you accomplish their goals.

Why Do People Hate Delegation?

Because delegation is hard. Managers often have little experience with delegation or have forgotten that they have the power to delegate. They are busy doing their job and don't know how to let go and let their employees take over. You can regain control of your team by using this model to get honest feedback on the progress of your projects, identify areas where delegation fails, and delegate.

What is delegation in management?

Don't think of it as a one-time event but a process that can be improved over time. Delegation is the art of inspiring your team to take ownership of the work by identifying their strengths and figuring out how to utilize their talents best to achieve the goals you set for them. The best experts in the delegation will admit that it is difficult to do, especially if you don't have experience with it. These are some of the steps you can take to get better at delegation and see better results from your team:

Identify The Task

First thing first: Before you delegate any work, you must identify what exactly needs to be done. This will make it easier to determine whether others can do the work and, if so, who you should assign to do the job.

Identify The Who and The How

Second, you must identify who you are delegating the task to. It is important to select someone with the skills needed to complete the task and someone with whom you feel comfortable having your teamwork. This will help ensure that your team members understand exactly what is expected of them and your expectations for their performance in performing that particular task.

Identify The Why

Third, you should identify the why. Why are you delegating this task? Simple: It will help motivate your team and provide understanding for your decision. For example, if it's an important task that must be done or the work is vital to the organization, you should assign it to someone who can do it well.

Establish Expectations and Rules of Engagement

Once you've identified what needs to be done and who/how it needs to be done, establish expectations on how they will complete the work. Delegating work means giving them authority to do it so they know what is expected of them. This can be achieved by creating timelines, providing instructions, or letting your team know you will be available if they have questions.

Offer Positive Feedback

This step may not seem necessary because most people believe that if you're delegating the tasks, then it's obvious what the outcome of the work should be. However, consider setting "little goals" and a completion time frame. This will help your team maintain motivation since they have something tangible to look forward to at the end of the process.

Characteristics of effective delegation

Successful delegation is not just a matter of title but also a matter of style. Several characteristics will help you achieve effective delegation. They can be summarized as follows:

1. Be available and willing to guide.
2. Set aside time for the process of delegation.
3. Be honest and don't "pass the buck" (delegate responsibility).
4. Offer continuing support after the delegation process is complete; this will keep a team from drifting apart and provide a venue for coaching/mentoring new team members assigned to your team.
5. Communicate openly so everyone knows what is happening within your workplace, especially if you delegate authority or responsibility for decisions to your employees (see below).

Elements of Delegation All Managers Should Know:

Managers should study and learn the three elements of delegation to apply them for the betterment of their organization.

1. Authority- The most important element of delegation is the authority you grant to your employees. This means recognizing they have the ability and the right to make decisions and implement their plans. This means your employees are self-motivated and don't need a boss telling them what to do, especially if they have been trained to work independently.

2. **Responsibility**- This means that you, as the manager, must be willing to recognize your employees for their success. If you truly believe in your employees, try to model the behavior you expect from them. Look at yourself in the mirror and ask yourself why you would want to delegate tasks to someone else if they were consistent and trustworthy.

3. **Accountability**- This means that you, as the manager, must take full responsibility for the outcome. You must ensure that employees are fully aware of their tasks and goals. You must hold each employee responsible for reaching these goals and accepting any failure due to poor performance.

These three elements will help managers oversee their employees more effectively, reduce management turnover and increase productivity.

How to delegate effectively

Delegation is the process of assigning work to someone else. There may be times when delegating work will be the best course of action, especially when it comes to getting a task done or completing a project that is important to your organization. However, there are certain aspects of delegation that you should take into careful consideration before you begin this process.

5 Tips for Delegating Effectively:

1. Be clear and concise – This can be difficult if you aren't used to delegating work, especially if a lot is on your plate already; however, if everyone knows exactly what they need to do and when it becomes easier for them to complete the tasks you have delegated.

2. Have realistic expectations – If you can't closely monitor the progress of the work you are delegating, consider creating a timeline with deadlines and milestones. This will help ensure your employees understand what is expected and how they can be available if they have questions regarding their work assignments.

3. Provide a structure for the work – As mentioned above, trying to monitor things closely may be difficult for many managers and business owners; however, you can still monitor the progress of your team members by providing structure and guiding them through the process of completing their tasks within this structure.

4. Provide positive feedback – Since this process is new for you, it may be difficult for your team to accept that you are delegating tasks t them. Providing positive and negative feedback is crucial so they can easily see the progress and specific tasks they are doing wrong.

5. Keep open lines of communication – After delegating your team, staying in contact with them regarding their progress on the project/task is important. This ensures that you can ask questions, see where they have fallen short or ensure everything is going well.

Three types of tasks you should be delegating

When delegating tasks, you should keep in mind that there are three types of tasks:

Routine and Administrative Tasks:

Routine and administrative tasks are typically repetitive and time-consuming and do not require high expertise or decision-making. These tasks include data entry, scheduling appointments, organizing files, and managing email correspondence. Delegating such tasks allows you to focus on more strategic and critical responsibilities, maximizing your productivity and effectiveness as a manager or leader.

Specialized or Technical Tasks:

Certain tasks require expertise or technical knowledge that may not be within your specialization. In such cases, delegating these tasks to individuals or team members with the necessary skills and experience is advisable. This could include graphic design, coding, financial analysis, or legal research. By delegating these specialized tasks to capable individuals, you can leverage their expertise and ensure that the work is done efficiently and effectively.

The Impact of Delegation on Team Performance

Delegation has a profound impact on team performance. It is not just about distributing tasks but also about empowering team members to take ownership of their work and make decisions. When managers delegate effectively, they create an environment of trust, responsibility, and autonomy that significantly boosts team morale and productivity.

Improved Efficiency and Productivity: When tasks are appropriately delegated, it allows for work to be done simultaneously, reducing project timelines and increasing overall productivity.

Enhanced Skill Development and Morale: Delegation provides team members with opportunities to learn new skills, take on fresh challenges, and enhance their professional development. This not only boosts individual capabilities but also team morale, as members feel valued and trusted.

Increased Innovation and Problem-Solving: Delegation empowers team members to approach tasks creatively and develop innovative solutions. With more autonomy, employees can experiment, think outside the box, and contribute diverse perspectives to problem-solving.

Effective Resource Management: Delegation allows for more effective use of resources, as managers can focus their time and energy on strategic tasks while team members work on other essential aspects of the project.

Better Decision-Making: When team members are given the authority to make decisions, they become more engaged and invested in their work. This increased responsibility can lead to better decision-making as they feel a sense of ownership over the tasks and projects they manage.

How delegation empowers:

Delegation is not merely an exercise in task distribution; it's a powerful tool for empowerment, fostering an environment where team members can grow, learn, and innovate.

Promotes Autonomy: When managers delegate tasks to their team members, they grant them the autonomy to decide how best to accomplish those tasks. This sense of independence can boost their confidence, foster creativity, and encourage problem-solving.

Encourages Skill Development: Delegation provides team members with the opportunity to work on tasks that may not typically fall within their area of expertise, promoting skill development and cross-functional knowledge. This learning experience can increase their value to the team and the organization as a whole.

Fosters Trust and Respect: By entrusting tasks to team members, managers demonstrate trust in their team's abilities. This can enhance the manager's relationship with the team and cultivate a more collaborative, respectful, and supportive work environment.

Boosts Job Satisfaction and Morale: Delegation can significantly improve job satisfaction. When team members are given the chance to take on new responsibilities and challenges, they feel more engaged and valued, which can lead to a happier and more productive workforce.

Enhances Leadership Skills: Delegation provides an excellent opportunity for potential leaders within the team to demonstrate and hone their leadership skills. By taking on more responsibilities, these individuals can showcase their ability to manage tasks, make decisions, and guide other team members.

Improves Time Management: When managers delegate, they free up their own time to focus on more strategic, high-level tasks. This helps to better manage their workload and prevent burnout, while simultaneously giving team members the chance to contribute more significantly to the team's goals.

HOW TO START COACHING YOUR TEAM

Coaching is a fundamental skill that every leader must possess. It serves as a tool to motivate, guide, and help employees unlock their full potential and align their work with the company's goals. While it may be challenging at first, with the right approach, coaching can drive significant improvements in team performance and employee engagement.

First, let's start with understanding the concept of coaching.

Understanding Coaching and its Importance

In the workplace, coaching is a process where managers provide guidance and support to help employees improve their skills, performance, and growth. This process involves a series of interactions and communication, where managers act as facilitators to help employees find solutions, rather than providing solutions themselves.

Coaching is essential in today's dynamic work environment because it:

Improves performance: Regular coaching can help employees improve their performance by providing them with the skills, knowledge, and guidance they need to excel in their roles.

Enhances skill development: Coaching helps employees develop and refine their skills, enabling them to perform their jobs more effectively.

Promotes personal growth: It supports employees' personal growth by encouraging them to step out of their comfort zones, take on new challenges, and strive for continuous improvement.

Increases engagement and satisfaction: Coaching helps build stronger relationships between managers and employees, leading to increased job satisfaction and engagement.

Coaching vs. Mentoring: Understanding the Difference

Coaching and mentoring, while both beneficial, serve different purposes and use different techniques.

Coaching is typically a short- to medium-term relationship focused on specific developmental areas or skills. The coach is an expert who helps the coachee improve their performance or develop specific skills.

On the other hand, mentoring is a longer-term relationship where the mentor provides guidance, advice, and support based on their experience and knowledge. The mentor's role is to share their wisdom and experiences to help the mentee navigate their career.

Understanding these differences can help managers choose the right approach to supporting their team members' development.

Practical Tips for Effective Coaching

Being an effective coach requires a balanced mix of skills, patience, and empathy. Here are some practical tips for managers looking to hone their coaching skills:

Active Listening: Actively listen to your team members to understand their perspectives, challenges, and aspirations. This involves not just hearing the words, but also understanding the underlying feelings and emotions.

Ask Open-Ended Questions: Asking open-ended questions encourages employees to think through challenges and find their solutions. This approach fosters problem-solving and critical thinking skills.

Provide Constructive Feedback: Constructive feedback is essential for growth. Ensure your feedback is specific, balanced, and aimed at helping the employee improve.

Set Clear Expectations: Clearly communicate what is expected from employees in terms of their performance and goals. This helps in reducing confusion and enhancing productivity.

Empower and Encourage: Empower your team members to take ownership of their tasks and make decisions. Encourage them to learn from their mistakes and celebrate their successes.

Coaching is an essential skill that every manager should master. By implementing these tips and strategies, managers can foster a positive learning environment that nurtures talent, drives performance, and contributes to the organization's success.

What Are Management Skills?

Management skills refer to the attributes, competencies, and abilities that individuals need to effectively manage, lead, and supervise others within an organization. These skills are critical for individuals in leadership and managerial roles as they determine how well they can guide their teams towards achieving organizational goals and objectives.

There are three primary types of management skills:

Technical skills: These are the specific abilities and knowledge needed to perform particular tasks or jobs. They can include skills in using certain software, project management methodologies, or industry-specific expertise.

Human or interpersonal skills: These are the skills needed to interact effectively with other people. They include communication, listening, conflict resolution, negotiation, and emotional intelligence.

Conceptual skills: These are high-level skills that involve the ability to understand complex situations and concepts, make strategic decisions, and envisage how different parts of an organization fit together.

These management skills work in conjunction to ensure a leader or manager can effectively guide their team and achieve the desired results.

What Is Coaching?

In the context of management, coaching refers to a one-on-one process where managers work with their team members to enhance their performance, develop new skills, and build their capabilities for future roles. It is a way of facilitating employees' professional growth and development by encouraging self-discovery, providing feedback, and challenging them to step out of their comfort zones.

Coaching is not about telling employees what to do or how to do it. Instead, it involves guiding them to discover the answers for themselves. This process enhances their problem-solving and critical thinking skills and increases their confidence in

Coaching is critical in the workplace because it can:

Improve employee performance: Through consistent feedback and guidance, employees can gain a better understanding of their strengths and areas of improvement.

Increase employee engagement: Employees who feel supported and valued by their managers are more likely to be engaged and committed to their work.

Promote personal and professional growth: Coaching encourages employees to continuously learn and grow, fostering a culture of continuous improvement.

Enhance team productivity: By improving individual performances, coaching indirectly leads to increased team productivity and effectiveness.

Effective coaching necessitates strong communication, active listening, empathy, and patience. By developing these skills, managers can become effective coaches, contributing significantly to their team members' growth and the organization's success.

6 Benefits Of Coaching For Managers

1. Add Depth To Your Knowledge

Coaching is not just about developing your team members; it is also an opportunity for you to learn and grow. As you help your employees navigate through their challenges, you will gain a deeper understanding of different aspects of your work, including industry trends, project details, and individual job roles.

2. Understand Your People

Coaching requires close interaction with your team members. It demands that you listen to their concerns, understand their motivations, and appreciate their strengths and weaknesses. Over time, this deep engagement helps you to understand your people better – their working styles, their aspirations, their fears, and their potential. This understanding can enable you to create a work environment where everyone feels valued and motivated.

3. Learn to Give Feedback

Feedback is a critical component of coaching. However, giving constructive feedback is an art that requires practice. As a coach, you need to learn how to give feedback that is honest yet motivating, specific yet respectful. Over time, this practice can help you master the skill of providing effective feedback – a skill that can significantly enhance your effectiveness as a manager.

4. Become A Manager Who Leads By Example

When you engage in coaching, you demonstrate your commitment to personal and professional growth – not just for your team members but for yourself as well.

This sends a powerful message to your team: that you value learning and growth, and that you practice what you preach. Thus, coaching helps you to become a manager who leads by example, inspiring your team members to strive for continuous improvement.

5. Bring Out the Best in Your Team

Effective coaching can help bring out the best in your team members. It can help them identify their strengths, overcome their weaknesses, and develop their potential. By helping them perform at their best, you can enhance the overall performance and productivity of your team.

6. Become an Indispensable Asset for Your Organization

As a manager who can effectively coach your team members, you become an indispensable asset for your organization. Your ability to develop people can help your organization build a strong talent pipeline, enhance team performance, and create a culture of learning and growth. In the long run, these contributions can significantly enhance your organization's competitiveness and success.

How To Start A Good Coaching Relationship With Your Employees?

Developing a successful coaching relationship with your employees is a process that requires time, effort, and a genuine commitment to their growth. It involves creating a supportive environment where employees feel valued, respected, and empowered.

This section provides an introduction to three fundamental strategies that can help managers to establish a strong coaching relationship with their employees.

1. Establish Trust By Demonstrating Sincerity

Trust is the bedrock of any coaching relationship. Employees are more likely to open up, share their concerns, and accept feedback if they trust their manager. To establish trust, you must demonstrate sincerity in your actions and communications.

2. Focus on Building A Rapport With Employees

Building rapport is about creating a connection with your employees. It involves understanding their perspective, respecting their ideas, and acknowledging their feelings. To build rapport, try to engage in regular, informal conversations with your employees. Ask about their interests, aspirations, and concerns.

3. Adopt A Flexible Approach

Every employee is unique, with different strengths, weaknesses, and learning styles. As such, a one-size-fits-all approach to coaching is unlikely to be effective. Instead, try to adopt a flexible approach that is tailored to the needs of each employee. For example, some employees may benefit from a more direct, hands-on style of coaching, while others may prefer a more collaborative, discussion-based approach. By being flexible and adaptable, you can ensure that your coaching efforts are as effective as possible.

Importance of Coaching Employees

Coaching plays a pivotal role in an organization's success by nurturing talent and fostering a culture of continuous learning. When managers coach their employees, they help them unlock their potential and bring out the best in them. This not only aids personal development but also increases their engagement and motivation, leading to enhanced job satisfaction and performance.

How to Coach Employees Effectively

Effective coaching starts with clear communication. Managers must be able to articulate their expectations, provide constructive feedback, and guide their employees towards their objectives. One-on-one meetings provide an ideal platform for this dialogue. During these meetings, managers should focus on the employee's performance, acknowledge their efforts, and discuss areas for improvement.

Active listening is another vital aspect of effective coaching. Managers should pay attention to their employees' ideas, concerns, and aspirations. This helps to build trust, show respect, and demonstrate that the manager values the employee's perspective.

Lastly, effective coaching involves facilitating the employee's growth rather than dictating it. Managers should help employees set realistic goals, identify the necessary resources, and create a plan to achieve them. This empowers the employee, giving them a sense of ownership over their progress.

The Differences Between Mentoring and Coaching

While both coaching and mentoring are valuable strategies for employee development, they serve different purposes and use different approaches.

Coaching is typically a shorter-term relationship focused on improving specific skills or behaviors. It is often task-oriented, with the coach providing guidance and feedback to help the employee improve their performance in a particular area.

In contrast, mentoring is usually a longer-term relationship, where the mentor provides guidance and advice to help the employee navigate their career. Mentoring is broader in scope than coaching and can encompass a wide range of areas, from developing leadership skills to understanding the organization's culture and politics.

While a coach typically has expertise in the area they are coaching in, a mentor does not necessarily need to have experience in the mentee's exact role. The mentor's role is more about sharing insights and experiences that can help the mentee make informed decisions and develop a broader perspective on their career.

The Skills Required for Mentoring

Mentoring requires a unique set of skills aimed at fostering personal and professional growth in a mentee. These include:

Empathy: Mentors must empathize with their mentees to understand their perspectives, struggles, and aspirations truly. This emotional understanding forms the foundation of a strong mentoring relationship.

Active Listening: Mentors must have excellent listening skills to fully understand their mentees' concerns and aspirations. Active listening involves not just hearing the words but also interpreting the emotions and meanings behind them.

Patience and Tolerance: Mentoring is a long-term commitment that may not show immediate results. Mentors need to be patient and tolerant as their mentees navigate their learning curves.

Critical Thinking: Mentors need to help their mentees solve problems and make decisions. This requires critical thinking skills to evaluate various situations and provide sound advice.

Communication: Effective mentoring requires clear, respectful, and open communication. Mentors should be able to provide feedback and guidance in a way that encourages and inspires their mentees.

The Skills Required for Coaching

Coaching, like mentoring, requires a distinct set of skills. These include:

Goal setting: Coaches must be adept at helping their coaches set specific, measurable, achievable, relevant, and time-bound (SMART) goals.

Observation: Coaches need to observe their coaches' performance to provide accurate feedback. This requires keen attention to detail.

Questioning: Effective coaches use powerful questioning techniques to encourage their coaches to think critically and find solutions to their problems.

Feedback: Coaches need to provide constructive feedback that encourages improvement without damaging confidence. They should highlight strengths, recognize achievements, and suggest ways to address weaknesses.

Motivation: Coaches should be able to motivate and inspire their coachees to reach their full potential.

The Key Benefits to Mentoring and Coaching

Mentoring and coaching both offer several benefits for individuals and organizations alike. These include:

Enhanced Performance: Both mentoring and coaching can improve performance by helping individuals develop their skills, boost their confidence, and navigate challenges effectively.

Career Development: Mentoring often focuses on long-term career development, helping individuals make informed career decisions, and develop leadership skills.

Increased Engagement: Individuals who receive coaching or mentoring typically show higher levels of engagement, leading to lower turnover rates and higher job satisfaction.

Cultural Development: Mentoring and coaching can help promote a culture of continuous learning and development within an organization, fostering a more positive, collaborative, and productive work environment.

Leadership Development: Both mentoring and coaching play crucial roles in developing future leaders. They help individuals gain the skills, confidence, and strategic insights they need to take on leadership roles effectively.

OVERCOMING RESISTANCE TO DELEGATION

While coaching and mentoring can be incredibly valuable to organizations, many leaders find it difficult to delegate tasks and responsibilities to their employees. There are several reasons why people resist delegation, including:

Lack of trust: One of the primary reasons why people refuse to accept delegated tasks is a lack of trust. Employees may feel that their managers do not trust their abilities or that they will be held responsible for any mistakes that occur. Building trust through open communication, providing clear expectations, and demonstrating confidence in employees' capabilities can help overcome this barrier.

Fear of job loss or reduced status: Some employees may fear delegating tasks to them as a sign that their manager is trying to replace them or reduce their importance within the organization. This fear can lead to resistance and reluctance to accept delegated tasks. Managers should emphasize the benefits of delegation, such as skill development and increased responsibility, to address these concerns.

Perfectionism: Individuals with a perfectionist mindset may find it challenging to delegate tasks because they believe that no one else can perform the task as well as they can. This mindset can lead to micromanagement and hinder the growth and development of team members. Managers can address this barrier by providing training and support to employees, demonstrating confidence in their abilities, and emphasizing the importance of shared responsibilities.

Lack of confidence or skills: Employees may refuse delegated tasks if they feel they lack the necessary skills or knowledge to complete them successfully. In such cases, training, guidance, and resources to build their confidence and enhance their skills can help overcome this barrier. Managers should communicate that delegation is an opportunity for growth and provide ongoing support and feedback.

Workload concerns: Employees may already have a heavy workload, making it challenging to accept additional tasks. They may resist delegation if they feel overwhelmed or believe the workload is unreasonable. Managers should consider employees' responsibilities and workload when delegating tasks, ensuring a fair distribution of work, and providing adequate support.

Lack of clarity and communication: Unclear expectations and poor communication about delegated tasks can lead to confusion and resistance. Employees may hesitate to accept tasks if they do not fully understand the objectives, timelines, or desired outcomes. Managers should provide clear instructions, communicate expectations, and encourage open dialogue to ensure mutual understanding.

Overcoming Barriers to Delegation

As individuals and organizations face more complex and challenging business environments, delegation becomes increasingly essential. It's crucial to overcome the barriers that prevent you from effectively delegating tasks to your employees by:

Understand your role as a leader: Managers and leaders may feel overwhelmed by meeting their team's daily needs and managing the details of their jobs. Recognize your role as a leader to help you overcome this challenge.

Take inventory and evaluate resources: Determine your team's strengths and weaknesses and assess resources to help you identify which tasks can be delegated. Determine whether there are specific areas you can delegate or ask a virtual assistant to handle.

Prioritize: Prioritizing this list will help you determine which tasks to delegate first and how much time the task will take from your employees. Use process mapping and the Eisenhower Matrix to organize and prioritize your employee's responsibilities. The Eisenhower Matrix examines a person's work, determines their strengths and weaknesses, and specific tasks that would be better left to others than subordinates.

Communicate the "why": As a leader, it is essential to communicate the "why" to your team. Make the time to talk with them about the benefits of delegation. This helps get employees on board, especially those with negative experiences with delegation, and why they should embrace this change.

Work together: The team must work together to delegate a task or project successfully. As leaders, you should create an environment where your team feels comfortable sharing ideas and guidance on completing tasks and assignments and when something may need more attention or support.

Set milestone meetings: Setting milestone meetings with your team is essential to ensure they are on track with a project and to review the progress. This will also allow you to give feedback, coach and mentor your employees, and move them forward when needed.

Recognize the work that has been done: When delegating a difficult task or project, help your employees review their accomplishments and give them the recognition they deserve.

Chapter Summary and Key Takeaways:

In this chapter, we've delved deep into the art of delegation and the essential skill of coaching. We have shed light on how these two management tools can empower a team, increase productivity, and foster a culture of trust and growth.

Using the Manager Tools Delegation Model, we've dissected the process of effective delegation, from selecting the right task and person, to setting clear expectations, providing training, and offering constructive feedback. Furthermore, we've addressed the hurdles that often prevent managers from delegating, and shared strategies to overcome these obstacles.

We also explored the invaluable skill of coaching. Distinguishing it from mentoring, we looked at how coaching can be an impetus for employees to reach their full potential and align their efforts with the company's goals. We've shared practical tips to establish a fruitful coaching relationship with your employees and shown how it can benefit both the manager and the team.

Despite the evident benefits, some resistance to delegation is expected. We've analyzed the most common barriers to delegation and ways to overcome them. Building trust, explaining the reasoning behind tasks, and recognizing completed work are all strategies that can encourage employees to accept delegated tasks willingly.

From the inspiring words of Howard Schultz to real-life experiences shared on Reddit, this chapter has provided practical guidance on how to navigate delegation and coaching as a manager, demonstrating that people are more than willing to take responsibility if they're given clear guidance and the authority to act.

But what happens when things don't go as planned? When conflicts arise and crises ensue? The next chapter, "Navigating Conflict and Crisis Management", explores these situations and offers insights on how to manage them effectively. By mastering conflict and crisis management, leaders can ensure the smooth functioning of their teams even in the face of adversity. Remember, great leadership is not just about success in easy times, but also about steering your team through challenges and coming out stronger on the other side.

CHAPTER 6
NAVIGATING CONFLICT AND CRISIS MANAGEMENT

> *"In crisis management, be quick with the facts and slow with the blame."*
>
> LEONARD SAFFIR, PUBLIC RELATIONS EXECUTIVE

RECOGNIZING AND HANDLING CONFLICTS

Workplace conflict is common in organizations, and if left unaddressed, it can significantly negatively impact productivity, employee morale, and the overall work environment. Employers must understand the causes of conflict and implement strategies to effectively manage and resolve these issues. By doing so, organizations can foster a more harmonious and productive workplace.

Conflict is a natural reaction to change. Employees may become frustrated when they perceive their concerns being ignored or discounted. Even high-performing employees may feel threatened when undergoing significant changes in the workplace. Conflict is often the result of issues that stem from egos and personalities.

Managing workplace conflict is essential for the success of any organization. Conflict can lead to decreased employee engagement, increased turnover, and reduced productivity.

Additionally, unresolved conflicts can create a toxic work environment, affecting employee morale and overall job satisfaction. Addressing conflicts promptly and effectively can help improve communication, enhance teamwork, and maintain a positive organizational culture. This chapter will examine what causes workplace conflict, various management methods, and how to minimize its occurrence during organizational change.

Employers play a crucial role in managing workplace conflicts. They should create a supportive, inclusive work environment that encourages open communication and collaboration. Employers must set clear expectations, provide training on conflict resolution skills, and establish channels for employees to voice their concerns. Employers should also lead by example, demonstrating professionalism, respect, and fairness in employee interactions. Employers must understand the causes of conflict and develop appropriate strategies to address it. In the workplace, a variety of different factors contribute to work conflicts.

While it is impossible to prevent all workplace conflicts, employers can mitigate their occurrence by developing processes or procedures that help employees resolve issues positively. Educating employees about this process can reduce stress and improve overall productivity.

Poor communication is one of the leading causes of workplace conflict. Misunderstandings, misinterpretations, and lack of clarity can lead to employee disagreements and tension. Effective communication is essential for preventing and resolving conflicts.

The most essential part of conflict management is effective communication. You can decrease their chances of acting out in conflict by effectively communicating with your employees.

Managers must establish open lines of communication with their employees. Regular meetings should be held to discuss potential conflicts and possible solutions.

These meetings also provide an opportunity for employees to voice any concerns they have about the work environment or plans.

Meetings should be well-planned and include a clear agenda to reduce confusion or misunderstanding between participants. When possible, managers should incorporate a cross-functional approach to resolving workplace disputes, ensuring that the actions taken are supported by multiple stakeholders (e.g., business leaders, HR professionals).

Employers can implement the following strategies to improve communication:

Encourage open dialogue: Create an environment where employees feel comfortable expressing their thoughts and concerns. Encourage open dialogue and active listening.

Foster clear and transparent communication: Communicate employee expectations, goals, and objectives. Provide regular updates and feedback to ensure everyone is on the same page.

Practice active listening: Encourage employees to listen to one another actively, seek to understand different perspectives, and avoid making assumptions.

Use nonviolent communication techniques: Teach employees to communicate assertively, expressing their needs and concerns without aggression or hostility. Focus on "I" statements and use non-blaming language.

Metrics and Reporting

Another cause of workplace conflict is a lack of awareness and transparency. When employees do not have visibility into specific policies or performance metrics, they may develop the perception that they are being treated unfairly.

Metrics are the systems that allow us to measure the performance of an organization or a department. These metrics can be financial indicators (such as sales, profit margins, return on investment, etc.), customer behavior (like customer satisfaction), employee engagement (such as employee turnover rate), or any other indicator that is important for your business (like support ticket response time). Metrics reporting helps to track progress and identify improvements over time. It creates a transparent environment where everyone can see how they are doing in completing their goals and objectives. Metrics and reporting are the primary way to measure the performance of an organization or department.

The effectiveness of these metrics is affected by the transparency of data and how it is reported. Everyone needs to clearly understand how reported data will be used, who will be controlling it, and when it will be updated. Just because employees agree with using metrics and reporting does not mean they are being used productively.

To avoid this issue, it's crucial to include all employees (especially those responsible for reporting) when developing metrics, so they can make sure that they don't inadvertently sabotage their departments' efforts through poor communication or misinterpretation of reporting guidelines.

Tracking and reporting conflicts can provide valuable insights for organizations to identify patterns, address systemic issues, and implement preventive measures. Employers can better understand the underlying causes by collecting and analyzing conflict-related data and taking appropriate actions. Some metrics and reporting practices to consider include:

Conflict incident reports: Establish a system where employees can report conflicts anonymously or confidentially. Analyze these reports to identify common triggers and trends.

Exit interviews and surveys: When employees leave the organization, conduct exit interviews or surveys to understand if conflicts played a role in their decision. Analyze this feedback to identify areas for improvement.

Employee feedback mechanisms: Implement regular employee feedback mechanisms such as surveys, suggestion boxes, or town hall meetings to gather insights on potential conflicts or areas of concern. Use this feedback to address issues proactively.

Causes of Conflict in the Workplace

Several factors can contribute to conflicts in the workplace. Understanding these causes can help employers identify potential issues and implement strategies to prevent or manage conflicts effectively. The leading causes of workplace conflict include:

Poor communication: Miscommunication, clarity, and misunderstandings can lead to conflicts. When information is not effectively conveyed or received, it can create tension and friction among employees.

Power struggles: Conflicts often arise when the organization has perceived or actual power imbalance. Competing for authority, resources, or recognition can result in conflicts and interpersonal tensions.

Personality clashes: Differences in personalities, work styles, and values can lead to conflicts. Employees with incompatible personalities or conflicting ways of working can create friction and hinder collaboration.

Role ambiguity: Unclear job responsibilities, overlapping roles, or conflicting expectations can lead to employee conflicts. When individuals are uncertain about their roles or have conflicting directives, it can cause tension and confusion.

Organizational change: Major changes such as restructuring, mergers, or leadership transitions can create employee uncertainty and anxiety. This can lead to conflicts as individuals adapt to new roles, processes, or organizational cultures.

Managing Conflict: Five Top Tips

When conflicts arise, it is essential to address them promptly and effectively. Here are five practical tips for managing workplace conflicts:

Stay calm and composed: It is crucial to remain calm and composed when faced with conflict. Avoid reacting impulsively or emotionally. Take a moment to gather your thoughts and approach the situation with a level-headed mindset.

Listen actively: Listening to the concerns and perspectives of all parties involved is key to resolving conflicts. Allow each person to express their viewpoint without interruption and demonstrate empathy and understanding.

Find common ground: Find areas of agreement or shared interests to find a resolution. Encourage collaborative problem-solving and explore win-win solutions that address the needs and concerns of all parties involved.

Seek mediation or HR assistance if necessary: If conflicts persist or escalate, involving a neutral third party, such as HR or a professional mediator, may be helpful. They can facilitate constructive dialogue, offer unbiased perspectives, and help parties find common ground.

Address conflicts early on: Don't let conflicts linger or escalate. Address them early, preferably at the first signs of tension or disagreement. Prompt action can prevent further escalation and minimize the negative impact on individuals and the organization.

Workplace conflict can have detrimental effects on organizations if left unaddressed. Employers should proactively address conflicts by promoting effective communication, providing conflict resolution training, and implementing clear policies. They should encourage a positive work environment, actively listen to employees, and seek mediation or HR assistance when needed. By addressing conflicts early on and taking appropriate actions, organizations can foster a harmonious and productive workplace that benefits employees and the business's overall success.

LEADING THROUGH A CRISIS

What are crises in an organization?

Crises are an inevitable aspect of any organization. Whether it is a small business or a multinational corporation, crises can occur anytime, anywhere, and without warning. A crisis can be defined as any significant occurrence that threatens an organization's normal operations. It can happen due to internal forces, such as poor decision-making, or external factors, such as natural disasters and accidents. A crisis can also be defined by its results, such as negative financial impact, loss of customers and employees, reputation damage, and media attention.

While it is impossible to avoid crises in almost every aspect of life, from personal relationships to politics and business, there are ways to make crises easier, specifically for those with leadership roles. Observing the factors involved in crisis management can teach one how to handle them properly when unavoidable.

The most critical aspect of a crisis is its potential to cause harm to people, property, and reputation. Organizations must act quickly to minimize the damage and prevent further escalation when a crisis occurs. Effective crisis management requires a well-planned and coordinated response involving all stakeholders, including employees, customers, suppliers, and the community.

Types of Crises in the Workplace

There are many ways in which crises can arise, but it is important to be aware of the different types of crises that frequently crop up in the workplace. A crisis can be either organic or man-made. An organic crisis is a natural event that occurs naturally and in which no one person is directly involved.

Examples of organic crises include raging forest fires, floods and droughts, earthquakes, and other natural disasters. A man-made crisis occurs when actors are directly responsible for causing it to happen. Examples of man-made crises include accidents, medical emergencies, crimes, and acts of terrorism.

Technological crises are caused by anything that contributes to the systemic failure of technology. An example of a technological crisis is the outage of an important technological system, such as an IT failure or power outage. Such a crisis can also be caused by cyber-attacks and data breaches, which compromise the confidentiality and security of data. Another form of technological crisis occurs when an organization uses technology in such a way that it causes physical harm to people, animals, property, or the environment. One recent example was when Uber allowed passengers to use its app to hail self-driving cars, which led to an accident.

Financial crises occur when an organization cannot meet its obligations, particularly those due immediately. They can also occur when the regular operations of an organization cut into its ability to meet payments, such as late employee or supplier payments. Financial crises can arise from many sources, including fraud and corruption, natural disasters, poor decision-making, and budgetary constraints.

Reputation crises are often the most damaging and difficult to overcome since the harm caused by one has a lasting impact on how people perceive an organization. This can translate into a loss of business and customer loyalty. A reputation crisis can be brought about by a wide range of issues, including corporate scandals, environmental damage, or labor abuses.

Product crises occur when a product or service fails to meet an organization's or its customers' expectations.

The best example is the Tylenol case, where cyanide was accidentally added to pain relievers, killing dozens of people and affecting many others. Another example was in August 2010, when metal fragments were found in Nurofen painkillers, and McNeil Consumer Healthcare recalled one million packets of the product.

Leadership crises occur when a high-ranking member of an organization cannot lead the company effectively. Both internal and external factors can cause such crises. Internal factors include poor management decisions, conflicts within the hierarchy, and dysfunctional work culture. An external factor can be corruption, scandals, or failure to meet legal requirements.

Legal crises arise when an organization violates the law or violates regulations. These can range from small infractions to serious crimes and violations that put people, property, and reputation at risk. Legal crises often damage an organization and may result in a fine, closure, or even imprisonment for its staff. On September 11, 2001, terrorists hijacked four commercial airplanes, crashing them into the World Trade Center in New York City and the Pentagon in Washington D.C. A fourth plane crashed outside of Shanksville, Pennsylvania, when passengers fought back against the hijackers. Approximately 2,977 people were killed during this terrorist attack on American soil.

Types of crisis management strategies

There are different types of crisis management strategies that organizations can use to navigate through difficult times. The choice of strategy depends on the type of crisis, the severity of the situation, and the resources available. Here are some of the most common crisis management strategies:

- **Reactive strategy** involves responding to a crisis, focusing on immediate containment, and minimizing the damage.
- **Proactive strategy** - This strategy involves anticipating potential crises, developing contingency plans, and building resilience within the organization to mitigate the impact of a crisis.
- **Preventive strategy** identifies and addresses potential risks and vulnerabilities before they escalate into a crisis. It involves implementing risk management practices, conducting regular assessments, and establishing protocols to prevent crises.
- **Damage control strategy** - This strategy aims to minimize the negative consequences of a crisis and restore normalcy as quickly as possible. It involves addressing the crisis, communicating transparently with

stakeholders, and implementing recovery plans.

- **Recovery strategy** - This strategy focuses on the long-term recovery and rebuilding of the organization after a crisis. It involves assessing the damage, identifying areas for improvement, and implementing measures to prevent similar crises.

Each crisis management strategy has its strengths and weaknesses, and the effectiveness of a strategy depends on the specific context and nature of the crisis. In many cases, a combination of strategies may be required to manage a crisis effectively.

CRISIS MANAGEMENT

Crisis management is the process of planning, coordinating, and executing actions to respond to and recover from a crisis effectively. It involves a systematic approach to identify, assess, and mitigate the impact of a crisis on an organization's operations, reputation, and stakeholders. The goal of crisis management is to minimize the negative consequences of a crisis and restore normalcy as quickly as possible.

Effective crisis management requires strong leadership, clear communication, and decisive decision-making. It involves assembling a crisis management team, developing a crisis management plan, and implementing strategies to address the specific challenges posed by the crisis. The success of crisis management relies on the ability of leaders to stay calm under pressure, make quick and informed decisions, and take responsibility for their actions.

Crisis Management Model

One commonly used crisis management model is the "Crisis Management Life Cycle" model, which consists of four phases: pre-crisis, acute crisis, chronic crisis, and resolution. Let's explore each phase in detail:

Pre-crisis phase: This phase focuses on preparedness and prevention. It involves identifying potential risks, conducting risk assessments, developing crisis management plans, and building the necessary capabilities and resources to respond effectively to a crisis. During this phase, leaders should establish clear roles and responsibilities, train employees on crisis response protocols, and establish communication channels for rapid and effective communication.

Acute crisis phase: This phase represents the onset of a crisis. It requires immediate action to contain the crisis, assess the situation, and activate the crisis management plan. The key priorities during this phase are to ensure the safety of employees and stakeholders, gather accurate information about the crisis, and communicate transparently with internal and external stakeholders. Leaders must make quick decisions based on the available information, allocate resources effectively, and adapt the crisis management plan as needed.

Chronic crisis phase: If a crisis prolongs or escalates, it enters the chronic crisis phase. This phase involves managing the long-term effects of the crisis and working towards recovery. It requires ongoing monitoring of the situation, adjusting strategies and actions as necessary, and engaging in continuous communication with stakeholders. Leaders should assess the impact of the crisis on the organization's operations, reputation, and financial stability and implement measures to mitigate further damage and facilitate recovery.

Resolution phase: The resolution phase occurs when the crisis is under control, and the organization moves towards recovery and restoration of normalcy. This phase involves evaluating the effectiveness of the crisis management efforts, conducting post-crisis analysis, and implementing corrective actions and improvements to prevent similar crises. Leaders should communicate the actions taken to address the crisis, express gratitude to employees and stakeholders for their support, and focus on rebuilding trust and confidence.

Crisis Management Plan

A crisis management plan is a documented set of procedures and guidelines that outline how an organization will respond to and manage a crisis. It is a roadmap for leaders and employees to follow during a crisis, ensuring a coordinated and effective response. Here are the key components of a crisis management plan:

a) Risk assessment and scenario planning: Identify potential risks and vulnerabilities that could lead to a crisis. Conduct scenario planning exercises to anticipate different crises and develop response strategies.

b) Crisis management team: Assemble a dedicated crisis management team consisting of individuals from various departments and levels of the organization. Assign specific roles and responsibilities to each team member, ensuring clear lines of communication and decision-making.

c) Communication protocols: Establish clear communication channels and internal and external communication protocols during a crisis. Define who will communicate with employees, customers, suppliers, media, and other stakeholders. Develop templates for crisis communication messages to ensure consistency and accuracy.

d) Training and drills: Train employees on crisis response protocols and procedures. Conduct regular drills and simulations to test the crisis management plan's effectiveness and identify improvement areas.

e) Crisis response procedures: Outline step-by-step procedures for responding to crises. Include guidelines for assessing the severity of the crisis, activating the crisis management team, gathering information, making decisions, allocating resources, and communicating with stakeholders.

f) Resource allocation: Determine the resources required to manage a crisis effectively, including personnel, equipment, technology, and financial resources. Identify backup systems and alternative suppliers to ensure continuity of operations.

g) Media relations: Develop a media relations strategy to manage external communications and public perception during a crisis. Designate a spokesperson or team to handle media inquiries and prepare key messages to convey the organization's position and actions taken.

h) Business continuity planning: Create a business continuity plan to ensure the organization can continue operating essential functions during a crisis. Identify critical processes, establish backup systems, and prioritize activities to minimize disruption.

Crisis Communication

Effective communication is crucial during a crisis as it helps manage uncertainty, provide accurate information, and maintain stakeholder trust. Here are some key principles for effective crisis communication:

a) Transparency: Be transparent and honest in communicating information about the crisis. Provide timely updates, acknowledge any mistakes or shortcomings, and share the actions to address the crisis.

b) Consistency: Ensure consistency in messaging across different communication channels and spokespersons. Avoid contradicting information or mixed messages that can create confusion and erode trust.

c) Empathy: Show empathy and understanding toward the concerns and emotions of employees, customers, and other stakeholders. Address their needs and demonstrate that their well-being is a top priority.

d) Clarity: Use clear and concise language when communicating complex information. Avoid jargon or technical terms that may confuse or mislead the audience. Provide instructions or guidelines if necessary.

e) Multi-channel approach: Utilize multiple communication channels to reach different stakeholders effectively. This may include email, intranet, social media, press releases, and town hall meetings. Adapt the message format and tone to suit each channel.

f) Two-way communication: Encourage employee and stakeholder feedback, questions, and concerns. Create channels for them to share their thoughts and provide updates or responses to address their feedback.

g) Monitoring and response: Monitor social media and other channels for public sentiment and feedback. Respond promptly to any misinformation or negative comments to correct inaccuracies and maintain control of the narrative.

Crisis Management Team

The crisis management team manages the organization's response to a crisis. The team typically includes senior executives, department heads, and subject matter experts. Here are the key roles and responsibilities within a crisis management team:

Crisis management team leader: The team leader is responsible for overall coordination and decision-making during a crisis. They provide strategic direction, ensure the team works effectively towards the common goal, and communicate with senior management and other stakeholders.

Communications Coordinator: The communications coordinator manages all internal and external communication during the crisis. They develop and disseminate key messages, handle media inquiries, and ensure consistent and timely communication with employees, customers, suppliers, and the public.

Operations manager: The operations manager oversees the operational aspects of the crisis response. They assess the impact of the crisis on the organization's operations, coordinate resource allocation, and ensure business continuity. They work closely with department heads to address operational challenges and implement contingency plans.

Human resources manager: The human resources manager focuses on the well-being of employees during a crisis. They support and guide employees, address their concerns, and ensure their safety. They may also coordinate employee assistance programs, counseling services, and other resources to help employees cope with the crisis.

Legal advisor: The legal advisor provides legal counsel and guidance to the crisis management team. They assess the legal implications of the crisis, advise on compliance and regulatory issues, and help mitigate legal risks. They also coordinate with external legal counsel if necessary.

Finance manager: The finance manager handles financial aspects related to the crisis. They assess the financial impact of the crisis, manage financial resources, and ensure financial stability during the crisis. They may also work with insurance providers, investors, and other financial stakeholders to address financial implications.

Technology expert: The technology expert provides expertise in managing technological aspects of the crisis. They assess the impact of the crisis on the organization's IT infrastructure, cybersecurity, and data management. They work closely with IT teams to address technological vulnerabilities, restore systems, and protect sensitive information.

Each crisis management team member brings expertise and perspective to manage the crisis effectively. The team works collaboratively, sharing information, making decisions, and implementing strategies to mitigate the impact of the crisis and ensure a swift recovery.

Ways to Overcome Crisis

Overcoming a crisis requires strategic thinking, effective decision-making, and strong leadership. Here are some ways to navigate through a crisis:

a) Stay calm and composed: As a leader, staying calm under pressure and maintaining a composed demeanor is essential. This helps instill confidence in employees and stakeholders and enables clear thinking and effective decision-making.

b) Gather accurate information: During a crisis, it is crucial to gather accurate and reliable information about the situation. This involves staying updated through various channels, consulting experts, and verifying facts before making decisions.

c) Assess the impact: Understand the potential impact of the crisis on the organization, its employees, customers, and other stakeholders. Assess the severity of the crisis and prioritize actions based on the level of threat and urgency.

d) Communicate transparently: Transparent communication is key to maintaining trust and managing uncertainty during a crisis. Keep employees and stakeholders informed about the situation, actions, and any changes or developments. Address concerns and provide reassurance whenever possible.

e) Make quick decisions: Crises often require quick decision-making due to urgency and rapidly evolving nature. Gather relevant information, consult with the crisis management team if necessary, and make informed decisions on time.

f) Delegate and empower: In a crisis, delegating tasks and empowering team members to take ownership of their responsibilities are essential. Distribute workload, assign roles and responsibilities, and provide the necessary resources and support for effective execution.

g) Take responsibility for mistakes: In a crisis, mistakes can happen. Leaders must take responsibility for errors, communicate openly, and take corrective action. Accountability and transparency are crucial in maintaining trust and credibility.

h) Learn from the crisis: After the crisis has been resolved, take the opportunity to reflect and learn from the experience. Conduct a post-crisis analysis to identify strengths, weaknesses, and areas for improvement.

Role of Employees in Crisis

Employees become crucial assets in navigating through uncertainty and turbulence during a crisis. They are the front-line representatives of the organization, directly engaging with customers, clients, and stakeholders.

Employees possess invaluable insights, expertise, and knowledge that can contribute to crisis resolution. Their roles during a crisis can include the following:

Crisis Communication: Employees are conduits for disseminating accurate and timely information to internal and external stakeholders. They can help manage rumors, provide updates, and address concerns, thus maintaining transparency and trust.

Operational Support: Employees play a significant role in ensuring critical operations continue despite the crisis. They adapt to new circumstances, adjust workflows, and collaborate to minimize disruptions and maintain business continuity.

Problem-Solving: Employees contribute their expertise and skills to identify innovative solutions to challenges arising from the crisis. Their ability to adapt, think critically, and propose alternative approaches is invaluable in overcoming obstacles.

Emotional Support: Employees may require emotional support during crises, particularly when they face personal or professional challenges. Encouraging a supportive work environment, providing resources for well-being, and promoting open communication channels are vital for maintaining employee morale and resilience.

Role of Leaders in Crisis Management

Leadership is crucial in crisis management, setting an organization's tone, direction, and actions during challenging times. Effective leaders demonstrate certain characteristics and perform specific roles to guide their teams through crises:

Strategic Decision-Making: Leaders analyze the situation, evaluate risks, and make well-informed decisions prioritizing the organization's interests. They consider short-term and long-term consequences, weigh available options, and choose the most suitable action.

Clear Communication: Leaders must convey information promptly and transparently to ensure that employees, stakeholders, and the public are well-informed. By maintaining open lines of communication, leaders foster trust, reduce uncertainty, and facilitate coordinated efforts.

Empathy and Support: Leaders recognize the impact of a crisis on their employees and demonstrate empathy and support. They listen to concerns, provide reassurance, and address individual needs to foster a sense of security and trust.

Collaboration and Team Building: Leaders promote a collaborative environment, encouraging teamwork and collective problem-solving. By leveraging the strengths and expertise of their teams, leaders can effectively address complex challenges and enhance organizational resilience.

Effective communication of organizations during Crises

Effective communication is vital during crises, as it directly influences the perception and reputation of the organization. Here are some reasons why organizations must communicate effectively:

Crisis Response and Recovery: Prompt and transparent communication ensures stakeholders know the situation and the organization's response. It allows organizations to control the narrative, correct misinformation, and outline recovery plans, instilling stakeholder confidence.

Stakeholder Engagement: Effective communication engages stakeholders, including employees, customers, investors, and the public. It demonstrates the organization's commitment to addressing concerns, listening to feedback, and involving stakeholders in decision-making.

Maintaining Trust and Reputation: Crises can significantly erode trust and damage an organization's reputation. Effective communication helps rebuild trust by demonstrating transparency, accountability, and a commitment to resolving the crisis. It allows organizations to convey their values, intentions, and actions, protecting their reputation.

Managing Rumors and Misinformation: Without accurate information, rumors and misinformation can spread rapidly during a crisis. Effective communication helps counteract these by providing verified updates, clarifying misconceptions, and ensuring stakeholders access reliable information.

Employee Engagement and Morale: During a crisis, employees may experience heightened anxiety, fear, and uncertainty. Effective communication gives them the necessary information to understand the situation, make informed decisions, and feel supported. It fosters a sense of belonging, engagement, and motivation, contributing to employee well-being and organizational resilience.

Chain of Command and Crisis Leadership in Corporates:

Chain of Command, Business Continuity Planning, and Crisis Leadership in Corporates:

From the above information, it can be concluded that the chain of command and business continuity are important factors in any crisis. Crisis leadership is very important in handling a crisis for an organization.

Chain of Command: The chain of command indicates who reports to whom and who's responsible for which task. It indicates an organization's hierarchy and helps employees perform their work efficiently. In a crisis, it becomes very important as it helps to send the information up well-prepared and simultaneously communicate to bottom-level employees, which is crucial in a crisis. It enables everyone involved to make quick decisions and take timely action.

Business Continuity Planning: BCP is an organization's procedure to ensure business continuity following a disaster or crisis. It consists of three elements – IT recovery, Business Recovery, and Business Interruption Management. With these plans, the organization can perform well despite an unexpected calamity.

The objective of BC planning is to provide the capability for critical operations and services to continue during a disruption event until normal operations can resume.

It can be formal or informal and is often part of an overall Disaster Recovery Planning (DRP) process, including testing and exercises. The goal of any BCP is to facilitate the capability to continue operations during a disruption.

Crisis Leadership: Crisis leadership is one of the most important aspects of dealing with organizational crises. It is a set of skills that deals with issues that arise during a crisis. Establishing a solid plan is the first step toward creating an effective crisis management strategy. The key to managing crises and handling them successfully lies in crisis management leadership; this includes developing and implementing strategies for handling unexpected events and consistently maintaining the appropriate level of readiness for their anticipated impact.

The Surprising Ways Crisis Management Impacts Individuals:

Crises can have a significant impact on individuals both physically and mentally. People experience many emotions during and after a crisis, including anxiety, fear, anger, guilt, sadness, and depression. Surprisingly, the crisis can also impact individuals in positive ways, such as:

a) Increased Resilience: Going through a crisis can build resilience in individuals. It challenges them to adapt, think creatively, and develop problem-solving skills. Individuals gain confidence and become better equipped to handle future crises by overcoming challenges.

b) Opportunities for Growth: Crises often present personal and professional growth opportunities. Individuals may be called upon to take on new roles, learn new skills, or demonstrate leadership capabilities. These experiences can enhance their capabilities, broaden their perspectives, and accelerate their career development.

c) Strengthened Bonds: Crises can unite people, fostering stronger bonds and team collaboration. The shared experience of overcoming a crisis can create a sense of camaraderie and solidarity, resulting in stronger relationships among colleagues.

d) Increased Engagement: Individuals often feel a heightened sense of purpose and engagement during a crisis. The urgency and significance of the situation can motivate individuals to go above and beyond their regular duties, leading to increased productivity and dedication.

When Companies Deal with Crises Well, Individuals Notice, and Companies Benefit:

Individuals who have had positive experiences with a company during a crisis are more likely to be loyal customers, provide referrals, and recommend the company to others. Companies can reinforce this loyalty by providing employees with meaningful opportunities to express their concerns, ask questions, and identify ways the organization could improve its response.

Here are some ways in which individuals and organizations benefit:

Enhanced Reputation: Effective crisis management enhances the reputation of an organization. Individuals perceive the organization as trustworthy, responsible, and capable of handling challenging situations. A positive reputation can attract customers, investors, and top talent, contributing to long-term success.

Improved Employee Loyalty and Retention: Employees who witness effective crisis management develop loyalty and trust toward the organization. They feel valued, supported, and confident in the organization's ability to navigate future crises. This, in turn, increases employee retention rates, as individuals are more likely to stay with an organization they perceive as competent and reliable.

Increased Customer Trust and Loyalty: Customers appreciate organizations that handle crises well. When companies communicate effectively, address concerns, and take decisive action to resolve the crisis, customers develop a higher level of trust and loyalty. Satisfied customers are more likely to continue doing business with the organization and recommend it to others.

Positive Public Perception: Effective crisis management generates positive publicity for an organization. Media coverage highlighting the organization's swift and effective response can significantly improve its public image. This positive perception can attract new customers, investors, and partnerships, contributing to the organization's growth and success.

Competitive Advantage: Organizations that demonstrate their ability to handle crises effectively gain a competitive advantage over their peers. Potential customers and clients are more likely to choose a company they perceive as resilient and capable of managing unforeseen challenges. This advantage can lead to increased market share and business opportunities.

Learning and Continuous Improvement: Crises provide valuable lessons for organizations. By analyzing their response and outcomes, companies can identify areas for improvement and enhance their crisis management strategies. This continuous learning and improvement process strengthens the organization's ability to handle future crises and adapt to changing circumstances.

Organizations can enhance their reputation by effectively managing crises, building trust with stakeholders, and creating a resilient and adaptive culture. Individuals, in turn, benefit from personal growth, increased engagement, and a positive work environment. Ultimately, organizations that deal with crises effectively gain a competitive advantage, leading to long-term success and sustainability.

POST-CRISIS RECOVERY AND LESSONS LEARNED

Stages of crisis

The stages of a crisis, often referred to as the crisis lifecycle or crisis management continuum, describe the different phases a crisis typically goes through. These stages help understand a crisis's progression and guide crisis management efforts. Let's expound on each of the stages you mentioned:

Stage 1: Prodromal (Pre-Crisis):

The prodromal stage is characterized by warning signs and indicators that precede an actual crisis. During this stage, organizations may detect early signals or potential threats that could escalate into a crisis if not addressed. These warning signs could include financial instability, declining performance, employee dissatisfaction, customer complaints, or emerging industry trends. Recognizing and responding to these warning signs effectively can help prevent or mitigate the impact of a crisis.

Stage 2: Acute (Crisis):

The acute stage, or crisis stage, is when the crisis peaks. This stage is marked by a sudden disruption or event that threatens the normal functioning of an organization or community. The crisis becomes apparent and demands immediate attention and action. Examples of crises in this stage include natural disasters, industrial accidents, product recalls, data breaches, or public scandals. Crisis management efforts focus on containing the crisis, ensuring the safety of individuals involved, and minimizing the negative consequences.

Stage 3: Chronic (Clean-Up):

The chronic stage occurs after the acute crisis has been contained or stabilized. During this phase, organizations shift their focus from immediate response to long-term recovery and restoration. The emphasis is on cleaning up the aftermath, repairing damaged systems, and returning to normalcy. This stage may involve extensive efforts such as repairing infrastructure, managing legal and financial implications, addressing public relations concerns, and supporting affected stakeholders. The duration of the chronic stage can vary depending on the nature and severity of the crisis.

Stage 4: Crisis Resolution (Post-Crisis):

The crisis resolution stage marks the conclusion of the crisis and signifies the transition to a new normal. In this stage, organizations evaluate the lessons learned from the crisis and implement changes to prevent similar incidents in the future. Crisis resolution involves conducting thorough post-crisis analysis, identifying strengths and weaknesses in the crisis response, and implementing improvements in crisis management plans and procedures. It also includes communication efforts to restore the organization's reputation, regain stakeholders' trust, and ensure a smooth transition back to regular operations.

It's important to note that the stages of a crisis are not always strictly linear, and there can be overlap or cycling between stages depending on the complexity of the crisis. Effective crisis management involves preparedness, proactive monitoring of potential crises, swift response during the acute stage, thorough recovery efforts in the chronic stage, and continuous learning and improvement in the post-crisis stage.

Post-Crisis Stage

The post-crisis stage refers to the period after the immediate crisis has been resolved or mitigated. It is a time when organizations shift their focus from emergency response to recovery and rebuilding. During this phase, the primary goal is to restore normalcy, rebuild trust and confidence, and address any lingering effects of the crisis. The post-crisis stage typically involves assessing the impact of the crisis, conducting a post-mortem analysis to learn from the experience, and implementing measures to prevent similar crises in the future.

Organizations need to develop a comprehensive plan for post-crisis rebuilding to navigate the post-crisis stage. This plan should outline the steps and strategies required to restore operations, rebuild stakeholder relationships, and regain public trust. Some key considerations for a post-crisis rebuilding plan may include:

a) **Assessing the damage:** Conduct a thorough assessment of the impact caused by the crisis, including financial losses, reputational damage, and operational disruptions. This assessment will help in prioritizing recovery efforts and allocating resources effectively.

b) Communication and stakeholder management: Develop a communication strategy to rebuild trust and confidence among stakeholders, including employees, customers, suppliers, and the general public. Provide regular updates on recovery efforts, acknowledge shortcomings, and demonstrate a commitment to improvement.

c) Operational restoration: Develop a roadmap for restoring normal operations and resuming business activities. This may involve repairing infrastructure, replenishing inventory, rehiring staff, or implementing contingency plans to minimize future disruptions.

d) Learning and improvement: Conduct a post-mortem analysis of the crisis to identify lessons learned and areas for improvement. This analysis should examine the organization's crisis response strategies, communication protocols, and decision-making processes. Implement changes based on these findings to enhance crisis preparedness for the future.

Golden Rules for Crisis Management

While every crisis is unique, some fundamental principles, often called the "golden rules," can guide effective crisis management. Here are some key golden rules to consider:

Preparation is key: Invest in proactive crisis preparedness by developing comprehensive crisis management plans, conducting regular training and simulations, and identifying potential risks and vulnerabilities in advance.

Clear communication: Establish effective communication channels and protocols for disseminating timely and accurate information during a crisis. Transparency, honesty, and empathy should be emphasized to maintain trust and credibility.

Decisive leadership: Strong and decisive leadership is crucial during a crisis. Leaders should make timely decisions based on available information, consider the potential impact of their actions, and communicate their decisions clearly to the entire organization.

Collaborative approach: Foster collaboration and teamwork across departments and stakeholders. Encourage open communication, information sharing, and coordination to ensure a unified response to the crisis.

Agility and adaptability: Crises often require flexibility and the ability to adapt to rapidly changing circumstances. Organizations should be prepared to adjust their strategies and tactics to manage the crisis effectively.

Learn and improve: After the crisis has passed, conduct a thorough evaluation of the response to identify areas for improvement. Implement changes to policies, procedures, and crisis management plans based on lessons learned to enhance future resilience.

Remember that these golden rules serve as general guidelines, and each crisis may require tailored approaches based on the specific circumstances and nature of the organization.

Chapter Summary and Key Takeaways:

In Chapter 6, we navigated the complex landscapes of conflict and crisis management. We delved into the causes of conflict in the workplace, from poor communication and power struggles to personality clashes. By recognizing these triggers, leaders can address conflicts promptly, reducing the potential for escalation. We also examined ways to handle conflicts efficiently, stressing the importance of calm, active listening and finding common ground.

Equipped with conflict resolution skills, we turned to the challenge of crisis management. We explored different types of crises and how a leader can effectively steer the team during such times. With examples of companies that successfully managed crises, we illustrated the power of clear communication, quick decision making, and taking responsibility.

Finally, we looked at the post-crisis phase, emphasizing the necessity to reflect on experiences and lessons learned. By examining past crises, leaders can identify areas of improvement and strategize to prevent similar future situations.

We highlighted the significance of recovery plans and post-crisis rebuilding, which ensure the continuity and growth of the organization. But leading in today's dynamic world is not just about resolving conflicts and managing crises. The ability to drive change and tackle emerging leadership challenges is crucial. As we turn to Chapter 7, "Driving Change and Addressing Modern Leadership Challenges", we'll discuss leading change in the era of digital transformation, dealing with the challenges of remote work, and navigating the expectations of the new generation workforce. This next chapter will empower you to embrace change and turn challenges into opportunities. Remember, the best leaders not only adapt to change, they drive it.

CHAPTER 7
DRIVING CHANGE AND ADDRESSING MODERN LEADERSHIP CHALLENGES

> *The challenge of leadership is to be strong but not rude; be kind but not weak; be bold but not a bully; be humble, but not timid; be proud, but not arrogant; have humor, but without folly"*
>
> JIM ROHN

UNDERSTANDING CHANGE MANAGEMENT

What is change management

Change management is the process of coordinating people and resources, collectively known as human factors, to achieve the desired objectives of an organization. This process starts with foresight and planning and ends with deploying new strategies, structures, and initiatives effectively. The aim is to enable organizations to sustain successful business operations in line with changing market dynamics. In this regard, managers are called upon to implement various change initiatives in various departments of an organization.

It is virtually impossible to learn about and master every aspect of human factors in a short period. Thus, planning and implementing effective change management initiatives is imperative to increase productivity, efficiency, and customer satisfaction.

A successful change management initiative requires employees to adapt new processes, roles, values, and behaviors within their departments and work with others across the organization to achieve company-wide goals. An organization must adopt an inclusive approach to encourage employee participation to succeed in changing times.

Change management is a very important part of business operations that managers should handle professionally. It initiates the whole process for many businesses, including the marketing aspects. It recognizes that change is about implementing new systems or processes and supporting individuals and teams in embracing and adapting to change. It involves understanding the impact of change on people, addressing their concerns and resistance, and helping them develop the necessary skills and mindset to thrive in the new environment.

Effective change management requires clear communication, stakeholder engagement, and collaboration across all levels of the organization. It involves creating a shared vision, setting achievable goals, and outlining a roadmap for change implementation. Change management is not a one-time event but a continuous process focusing on managing the transition and ensuring the desired outcomes.

How does change management work?

Change management follows a structured approach to facilitate successful change implementation. It typically involves several key steps:

a. Assessing the need for change:

The change management process begins with a thorough analysis of the existing environment where the need for change is identified. This includes the issues that are creating bottlenecks and challenges facing organizations. For example, in many cases, organizations must make changes to address issues related to organizational goals, policies, and processes.

b. Developing a strategy for change:

Change management requires an appropriate strategy for change implementation for different scenarios and environments. For example, in some cases, organizational goals and objectives can't be achieved through a single process or initiative; thus, managers are expected to develop multi-faceted strategies for improving organization efficiency and effectiveness by applying new systems, processes, and initiatives.

c. Communicating the strategy for change:

After developing a strategy for change, it is necessary to communicate it to stakeholders (employees and management) at all levels and with relevant partners and suppliers. This is not only crucial in ensuring that there's a broad-based understanding of the organization's vision but also important in building support and commitment toward the change management process.

d. Selecting an implementation method:

An effective way of incorporating new strategies into the company's business operations is through selected "change agents" or "change managers." A change manager is a specific employee responsible for coordinating the implementation process and helping others for successful change uptake. The selection of the right change manager can be an important factor in ensuring that the desired outcomes are achieved.

e. Implementing change:

After selecting and training the right people and designing a strategy, change management comes into full-swing. The selected change agents are required to assist the organization's other employees adapt to new processes and systems.

f. Monitoring change:

After implementing new processes, systems, and initiatives, it is important to monitor them regularly so that they can be adjusted as needed while ensuring they're still effective in promoting goals and objectives. This allows managers to adjust strategy and technique until all stakeholders can adapt and have been successfully convinced about the benefits of new processes.

Change management for project management

Project management is crucial for organizations to succeed in the 21st century. Change management is particularly relevant in the context of project management. Projects often involve significant changes, whether in terms of processes, systems, or organizational structure. Incorporating change management practices into project management helps mitigate resistance, reduce disruptions, and increase the chances of project success.

The project manager must be strategic, disciplined, analytical, and well-organized to succeed. Good individuals with these qualities are easy to find, but the most difficult thing is to keep them motivated because their roles are so important inside and outside the organization. This role is known as change management or "change" because a large part of that person's time will be consumed by managing changes.

Good teams have a leader who can lead an organization and motivate individuals with change management at the same time.

Change management for project management involves:

a. Early identification of change impacts: By considering a project's potential impacts on various stakeholders, change management helps anticipate resistance and develop strategies to address it proactively.

b. Stakeholder engagement and communication: Involving stakeholders throughout the project lifecycle helps create a shared understanding of the project goals, benefits, and implications. Effective communication ensures stakeholders are informed, aligned, and supportive of the changes.

c. Training and skill development: Change management recognizes the importance of equipping employees with the necessary knowledge and skills to adapt to new processes or technologies. Providing adequate training and support helps minimize productivity dips and fosters a smooth transition.

d. Change control and risk management: Incorporating change management practices into project management includes monitoring and managing potential risks and changes. This involves assessing the impact of proposed changes, evaluating their alignment with project objectives, and making informed decisions about incorporating or rejecting them.

e. Celebrating successes and sustaining change: Recognizing and celebrating milestones and achievements throughout the project helps build momentum and maintain engagement. Moreover, sustaining change beyond the project's completion requires ongoing reinforcement, measurement of outcomes, and continuous improvement to embed the changes into the organization's culture and processes.

Types of Organizational change

Organizations can be structured in a variety of ways. There are five types of organizational change:

Strategic Change: This type of change focuses on the overall direction and goals of the organization. It involves significant shifts in the company's mission, vision, strategy, or structure to adapt to external factors or seize new opportunities.

Structural Change: Structural changes involve modifying the organization's framework, such as the hierarchy, reporting relationships, departments, or job roles. This change aims to improve efficiency, collaboration, or responsiveness to market demands.

Technological Change: Technological advancements often require organizations to adapt and implement new technologies or systems. This can involve upgrading existing systems, implementing new software, or adopting emerging technologies to enhance productivity, innovation, or customer experience.

Cultural Change: Cultural change transforms the organization's values, beliefs, norms, and behaviors. It aims to create a positive and inclusive work environment, foster innovation, improve employee engagement, or align the company culture with its strategic objectives.

Process Change: Process change involves modifying or reengineering existing business processes to streamline operations, eliminate inefficiencies, reduce costs, or enhance quality. It focuses on improving tasks and optimizing workflow to achieve better outcomes.

Popular Models for Managing Change

Lewin's Change Management Model

This model focuses on the impact of change on individuals and their varying levels of awareness. It is based on the work of Kurt Lewin, who proposed that an individual's perception of change is affected by their previous knowledge and experience with the change.

Additionally, this model identifies a handful of factors that may impact an individual's behavior regarding change (i.e., fear, anxiety, and resistance). It also proposes a three-step process for managing change: unfreezing (creating awareness and motivation for change), implementing change, and refreezing (reinforcing and stabilizing the change).

Kotter's 8-Step Change Model

Kotter's model emphasizes the need for organizations to shape a compelling vision and align their efforts to achieve it. It includes eight steps: (1) Establish a sense of urgency, (2) Create the guiding coalition, (3) Develop a vision and strategy, (4) Communicate the change vision, (5) Empower broad-based action, (6) Generate short-term wins or small successes, (7) Consolidate gains and produce more change initiatives, and (8) Sustain momentum.

ADKAR Model

This model promotes a more organizational approach to change management by helping organizations identify the various aspects of their operation (i.e., behavior, data, knowledge, attitude, and relationships) that need to be altered to achieve a state of equilibrium with the new change. It suggests that change can be achieved through a combination of "Awareness and belief in the need for change" (A), "Desire for the new state" (D), "Knowledge about how to make necessary changes" (K), "Ability to make necessary changes" (A), and "Rewards in place for desired behavior" (R).

Other tried-and-tested models are:

Bridges' transition model: William Bridges' model emphasizes the human aspect of change. It identifies three stages: an ending, a neutral zone, and a new beginning. Leaders need to help employees let go of the old ways, navigate the uncertainty of the transition, and embrace the new beginning.

Kübler-Ross change curve: Based on Elisabeth Kübler-Ross's work on grief and loss, this model describes individuals' emotional stages during change. The stages include denial, resistance, exploration, commitment, and acceptance. Leaders need to understand and address the emotional reactions of individuals to facilitate their transition.

Satir change management model: Developed by Virginia Satir, this model focuses on interpersonal relationships and communication during change. It emphasizes the importance of open and honest communication, building trust, and addressing individual concerns and needs.

PDCA change management strategy: The PDCA (Plan-Do-Check-Act) strategy, often associated with quality management, can also be applied to change management. It involves planning the change, implementing it, evaluating the results, and making necessary adjustments. This iterative process allows leaders to improve the change implementation continuously.

McKinsey's 7S change model aligns seven key organizational elements to ensure successful change. The elements include strategy, structure, systems, skills, staff, style, and shared values. Leaders using this model analyze and address each element to create a coherent and integrated approach to change.

The choice of a change management model depends on various factors, including the nature of the change, the organizational context, and the preferences and needs of the stakeholders involved. Each model has its strengths and limitations, and leaders should consider their specific circumstances when selecting a model.

Combining elements from different models or adapting existing models to fit the organization's unique needs may be beneficial. Flexibility and a customized approach are key to successfully applying change management models.

Benefits of Change Management

Change management supports organizational learning and innovation: Implementing effective change management practices helps organizations engage with and harness the power of creative thinking and innovative ideas. This approach provides a forum to adapt, adopt, or abandon new technologies or processes to remain competitive. Moreover, implementing change management helps create buy-in and support for new initiatives among employees, stakeholders, business partners, and the general public – strengthening organizational effectiveness and sustainability.

Change management fosters collaboration: Teamwork is integral to any project or task force where individuals work together to achieve common goals. Effective communication is critical in building trust between team members and aligning their visions toward achieving a shared goal. It is also important for team members to value one another's contributions and ensure each member has a voice in the decision-making process.

Change management promotes organizational effectiveness: Changing how people work, communicate, and interact can often result in greater efficiency and better results. A simple example is the timed coffee break, introduced at 3M, to increase worker focus on the job at hand while saving time and money on coffee supplies. The change involved changing attitudes (i.e., workers no longer considered taking a coffee break a luxury), adjusting behaviors (i.e., increased productivity and reduced employee fatigue), rethinking processes (i.e., using a time clock to track the number of coffee breaks taken), and altering systems (i.e., providing disposable cups and limited coffee supplies).

Change management encourages employee engagement: Employees who feel engaged with their jobs are more likely to be productive and perform at a higher level. Studies have shown that individuals who perceive they have some control over the events in their lives are less likely to experience stress or burnout and display greater professional commitment than those who lack this sense of control. Research also suggests that when employees believe they are empowered to make decisions about their work environment, organizations are more likely to benefit from increased productivity, enhanced performance quality, and greater profitability.

Change management helps reduce organizational risk: The complex nature of business transactions and transactions across boundaries often create risks for organizations, ranging from liability to the need for regulatory compliance. Change management can help businesses mitigate these risks by identifying potential issues, generating potential solutions, and testing proposed solutions in the field – all of which decrease the likelihood of getting sued or fined.

Principles of change management

Clear Vision and Objectives: Change management requires a clear understanding of the desired outcomes and involves setting them with urgency. This provides a sense of direction and purpose for the change initiative.

Effective Communication: Communication is crucial during times of change. Change managers must effectively communicate the reasons for change, the benefits, and the expected impact on individuals and the organization. Transparent and consistent communication helps to build trust and reduce resistance.

Stakeholder Engagement: Involving key stakeholders in the change process is essential for successful change management. Engaging stakeholders early on allows them to provide input, express concerns, and contribute to decision-making, fostering a sense of ownership and commitment to the change.

Change Leadership: Change management requires strong leadership that inspires and motivates employees throughout the change journey. Leaders should be role models, demonstrate commitment to the change, and support and guide their teams.

Resource Allocation: Sufficient resources, including financial, technological, and human resources, should be allocated to support the change effort. This ensures that employees have the necessary tools, training, and support to adapt to the change effectively.

Flexibility and Adaptability: Change is often accompanied by unexpected challenges and obstacles. Change management should embrace flexibility and adaptability to respond to these challenges and make necessary adjustments to the change plan as needed.

Popular Change Management Tools

Change Impact Assessment: This tool helps organizations assess the potential impact of a change on various aspects, such as processes, systems, employees, and stakeholders. It provides a structured approach to identifying and analyzing potential risks and enables organizations to develop mitigation strategies.

Change Readiness Assessment: This tool assesses the readiness of an organization or team to undergo a specific change. It helps identify strengths, weaknesses, and gaps in the organization's or team's ability to adapt to the change. Based on the assessment, appropriate interventions and support can be implemented to enhance readiness.

Change Communication Plan: A change communication plan outlines the communication strategy and tactics for the change initiative. It includes the target audience, key messages, communication channels, and the frequency and timing of communication. This tool ensures that relevant information is effectively disseminated to stakeholders throughout the change process.

Training and Development Programs: Training and development programs are essential to change management tools that help employees acquire the skills and knowledge required to adapt to the change. These programs can include workshops, seminars, e-learning modules, and on-the-job training to build competency and confidence in handling new processes or technologies.

Resistance Management Strategies: Resistance to change is common and change management tools should include strategies to address and overcome resistance. These strategies may involve active listening, involving resistant individuals in the change process, addressing concerns and misconceptions, and providing ongoing support and recognition for individuals who embrace the change.

Overcoming resistance to change

Sometimes, engaging in change management when there is resistance can backfire, as it will often fuel the resistance and reinforce negative beliefs about the organization. To successfully overcome resistance, change management teams may need to change which strategies they pursue or engage in. By switching strategies, change management teams might be able to lessen or even eliminate some of the damage caused by resistance to change.

For example, instead of persuading employees to embrace the changes, teams could try engaging them by addressing their concerns regarding performance and demonstrating their commitment to the organization. This approach would help give employees a sense of importance and control over their roles and responsibilities, which could help decrease resistance significantly.

Another approach is to address the resistance by addressing it with a focus on how the change will help employees and the organization. For example, a team may acknowledge that employees are concerned about their roles and responsibilities when changes are implemented but could then use this information to address whether these concerns are justified and work together to seek solutions.

There is no single change management technique that works for all organizations, but many of the strategies listed above may help improve organizational readiness for change and understanding how one's organization functions is essential for effective change management. Change management teams should look at their structure and processes to determine which changes they need to make to improve their readiness.

Change management is not just about convincing people to accept change, it is also about trying to understand why resistance exists in the first place. People do not resist for no reason; therefore, it may be a good idea for change management teams to explore the root causes of their resistance.

The main goal of this strategy is not to persuade individuals or teams that they should accept change but rather to try to get them to see things differently and understand that there are other ways in which they can benefit from the changes as well.

Resistance can be rooted in fear, anxiety, or stress. Try changing your perspective on what you present as negative and instead focus on the positive aspects of implementation.

How to prepare employees for changes

Preparing employees for changes is crucial to ensure smooth transitions and minimize resistance. Here are some key steps to consider:

a. Communication: Effective communication is vital during change initiatives. Clearly articulate the reasons for change, the benefits, and how it aligns with the organization's goals. Address concerns and provide opportunities for employees to ask questions and provide feedback.

b. Training and education: Identify the skills and knowledge gaps that may arise due to the change. Offer training programs or resources to help employees develop the required competencies. This can include workshops, seminars, online courses, or mentoring programs.

c. Involvement and engagement: Involve employees in the change process by seeking their input and participation. Encourage them to share their ideas, concerns, and suggestions. This involvement fosters ownership and commitment to the change.

d. Support systems: Provide support systems such as change management teams, mentors, or internal change agents. These individuals can offer guidance, address concerns, and assist employees in navigating the change.

e. Recognition and rewards: Acknowledge and reward employees who adapt well to change. Celebrate milestones and achievements to reinforce a positive mindset towards change.

Tips for successful change management

Implementing effective change management requires careful planning and execution. Consider the following tips:

a. Leadership commitment: Ensure leaders fully commit to and actively support the change. Their visible involvement and consistent messaging are crucial for inspiring confidence and fostering employee buy-in.

b. Clear objectives and milestones: Define objectives and break down the change process into achievable milestones. This provides a roadmap for progress and helps employees see the tangible outcomes of their efforts.

c. Stakeholder engagement: Identify and engage key stakeholders throughout the change process. Understand their concerns, involve them in decision-making, and keep them informed about the progress and impact of the change.

d. Flexibility and adaptability: Recognize that change may require adjustments. Stay flexible and adapt the change strategy based on feedback and emerging challenges.

e. Continuous communication: Maintain open and transparent communication channels throughout the change process. Regularly update employees on the progress, address concerns promptly, and provide a platform for feedback and suggestions.

f. Change champions: Identify change champions within the organization who can act as advocates and influencers. These individuals can help motivate and support their colleagues during the transition.

Top 10 reasons why you need a change management strategy

A change management strategy is essential for several reasons, including:

a. Minimize resistance: Change often triggers resistance from employees. A well-defined change management strategy helps identify potential sources of resistance and develop proactive measures to address them, increasing the chances of successful adoption.

b. Increase employee engagement: Involving employees in the change process fosters a sense of ownership and engagement. A change management strategy provides a framework to actively involve employees, encourage their input, and address their concerns.

c. Mitigate risks: Change initiatives can introduce various risks, such as disruptions to business operations or decreased employee morale. A change management strategy helps identify and mitigate these risks through proper planning, communication, and risk assessment.

d. Improve productivity and efficiency: Well-managed change minimizes disruptions and allows employees to adapt more quickly. This improves productivity and efficiency, as employees can focus on their work without prolonged uncertainty or confusion.

e. Enhance organizational agility: A change management strategy enables organizations to respond effectively to market changes, technological advancements, and evolving customer needs. It cultivates a culture of adaptability and agility, positioning the organization for long-term success.

f. Foster innovation: Change often drives innovation and encourages employees to think outside the box. A change management strategy provides a supportive environment that nurtures creativity and innovation, allowing new ideas to flourish.

g. Align with strategic goals: Change initiatives should align with the organization's vision. A change management strategy ensures that changes are implemented to support the organization's overall direction, maximizing the chances of achieving desired outcomes.

h. Enhance employee satisfaction: Employees feel valued and respected when actively involved and informed about changes. A change management strategy promotes transparency, open communication, and employee empowerment, leading to higher levels of job satisfaction.

i. Build resilience: Change is a constant in today's dynamic business environment. A change management strategy equips employees and the organization with the skills and mindset to adapt and thrive in the face of future changes.

j. Optimize resource allocation: Change initiatives often require resources such as time, budget, and personnel. A change management strategy helps optimize the allocation of these resources, ensuring they are utilized efficiently and effectively.

k. Strengthen organizational culture: Successful change management strategies reinforce the desired organizational culture. The strategy strengthens the overall culture and fosters employee loyalty and commitment by aligning changes with the organization's values and promoting a positive and inclusive work environment.

CHANGE LEADERSHIP

The 3 C's of Change Leadership

The 3 C's of Change Leadership are essential elements that leaders must incorporate into their change management strategies. These are Communication, Collaboration, and Creativity.

Communication involves effectively conveying the change's vision, mission, and objectives to all stakeholders. Leaders must communicate in a clear, concise, and compelling way to ensure everyone understands the change and their role in it.

Collaboration involves all stakeholders in the change process, from planning to implementation, to ensure everyone feels valued and committed to the change. Creativity involves thinking outside the box and encouraging innovation to find new and better ways to do things.

Becoming an Effective Change Leader

To become an effective change leader, you must first understand the change's reason, scope, and impact on the organization. You must also identify the stakeholders affected by the change and develop a clear vision and strategy for implementing the change. Effective change leaders also understand the importance of communication and involve stakeholders in the change process from the beginning. They provide training and support to ensure everyone understands their role in the change and has the necessary skills and resources to succeed.

Leading through the change process requires a leader to be proactive and take charge of the change process. They must identify potential obstacles and risks, plan for contingencies, and keep all stakeholders informed and engaged throughout the change process. Leaders must also create a sense of urgency around the change and be willing to make tough decisions when necessary. They must remain flexible and adaptable to changing circumstances and be willing to adjust their strategy as needed.

Leading people through change requires a leader to be empathetic and understanding of the emotional impact of change on employees. They must create a supportive and inclusive culture that encourages collaboration and innovation.

Leaders must also proactively address any resistance to change and provide the necessary training and support to help employees adapt to the new way of doing things. They must also recognize and reward employees for their efforts and contributions to the change process.

Great leaders drive change by creating a compelling vision that inspires and motivates others to embrace change. They communicate effectively, involve stakeholders, and provide the necessary resources and support to ensure everyone has the skills and tools to succeed. Great leaders also lead by example, demonstrating a willingness to embrace change and take calculated risks. They foster a culture of innovation and encourage employees to think outside the box and find new and better ways to do things.

Three Myths About Creating Change

Three common myths about creating change can hinder a leader's success. The first is that change can be achieved quickly and easily. Change is often complex and takes time and effort to implement successfully.

The second myth is that change can be imposed from the top down. Change must be a collaborative effort involving all stakeholders in the planning and implementation process.

The third myth is that change can be achieved through persuasion alone. Change requires a combination of persuasion, education, and practical support to succeed.

The truth about leading change is that it requires a multifaceted approach that incorporates elements of communication, collaboration, creativity, and flexibility. Leaders must be willing to take risks, make tough decisions, and adapt to changing circumstances to ensure the success of the change process.

Change leadership is a critical role that requires leaders to develop a clear vision, communicate effectively, involve employees, create a sense of urgency, and use change management models. By understanding the importance of their role, getting buy-in from employees, dealing with resistance, and fostering a culture that supports change, leaders can successfully navigate the complexities of change and drive positive outcomes for their organizations.

THE POWER OF ADAPTABILITY: BUILDING A RESILIENT WORKFORCE

Adaptability is critical in today's rapidly changing and unpredictable work environment. As organizations face new challenges and trends, adapting becomes crucial for individuals and managers.

Adaptability in the workplace refers to an individual or an organization's ability to adjust, change, and thrive in response to new challenges, trends, and circumstances. It involves being responsive and proactive rather than reactive when confronted with unexpected situations.

Adaptability encompasses flexibility, open-mindedness, and the willingness to embrace change and learn new skills. It is a personal attribute that enables individuals to cope with changing circumstances effectively. It involves embracing change and approaching new situations with a positive mindset. Individuals with adaptability skills are more likely to navigate challenges, learn from experiences, and seize growth opportunities.

Effective Strategies to Champion Change:

Embrace a Growth Mindset: Cultivating a growth mindset is essential for embracing change. It involves believing in one's ability to develop new skills and welcoming challenges as opportunities for personal and professional growth.

Foster a Culture of Learning: Encourage continuous learning within the organization. Provide opportunities for employees to enhance their knowledge and acquire new skills through training programs, workshops, and conferences. When employees feel supported in their pursuit of growth, they are more likely to adapt to change effectively.

Encourage Collaboration and Communication: Foster an environment that promotes collaboration and open communication. Encourage employees to share ideas, provide feedback, and work together to find innovative solutions. Collaboration allows for different perspectives and approaches to be considered, leading to more effective adaptation to change.

6 Important Workplace Adaptability Skills (With Examples):

Flexibility: Being open to new ideas and approaches and adjusting one's plans or strategies when necessary. For example, a manager who can quickly shift priorities to accommodate unexpected client requests demonstrates flexibility.

Problem-solving: The ability to analyze challenges, identify potential solutions, and take decisive action. A manager who can assess a problem and develop creative solutions to the root cause showcases strong problem-solving skills.

Resilience: The capacity to bounce back from setbacks and remain optimistic in adversity. An employee who can handle constructive criticism and use it as an opportunity for growth displays resilience.

Time Management: Efficiently managing one's time and priorities to meet deadlines and achieve goals. An individual who can adapt their schedule and allocate resources effectively in response to unexpected changes demonstrates strong time management skills.

Interpersonal Skills: Building positive relationships, collaborating, and effectively communicating ideas. Employees who adapt their communication styles to work effectively with different personalities showcase strong interpersonal skills.

Continuous Learning: The willingness to acquire new knowledge and skills to adapt to evolving job requirements. An individual who seeks out opportunities for professional development and actively stays updated with industry trends exhibits a commitment to continuous learning.

What are Adaptability Skills?

Adaptability skills are a set of abilities that enable individuals to adjust, learn, and thrive in changing environments. These skills include flexibility, problem-solving, resilience, time management, interpersonal skills, and continuous learning. Managers can effectively navigate new challenges and contribute to a resilient workforce by developing these skills.

Types of Adaptability Skills:

Cognitive Adaptability: The ability to process and assimilate new information quickly, think critically, and make informed decisions in rapidly changing situations.

Emotional Adaptability: The capacity to manage emotions and remain composed in stressful or uncertain circumstances. It involves maintaining a positive attitude and effectively dealing with change-related stress.

Behavioral Adaptability: The willingness and ability to modify one's behavior and approach based on the demands of a situation. This includes being open to feedback, adjusting work style, and embracing new ways of doing things.

Interpersonal Adaptability: The ability to work effectively with diverse individuals and adapt communication and collaboration styles accordingly. It involves being receptive to different perspectives and fostering positive relationships.

Analytical Thinking: The ability to analyze complex situations, identify patterns, and make data-driven decisions. This skill helps managers understand emerging trends and respond effectively.

Creativity and Innovation: The capacity to think creatively and generate innovative solutions. Managers who embrace new ideas and encourage creative thinking contribute to a more flexible and forward-thinking workplace.

Decision-Making: The ability to make sound decisions based on available information and on time. Managers who can weigh options, consider potential risks, and make decisive choices enable effective adaptation to change.

Leadership: Effective leadership plays a crucial role in driving organizational change and creating a culture of adaptability. Leaders who inspire and motivate their teams to embrace change contribute to a more resilient workforce.

How to Improve Adaptability Skills:

Embrace Continuous Learning: Actively seek out opportunities for personal and professional development. Attend workshops, conferences, and training programs to expand your knowledge and skills.

Step Out of Your Comfort Zone: Challenge yourself by taking on new responsibilities or projects that push you beyond your comfort zone. This helps build resilience and adaptability as you navigate unfamiliar territory.

Seek Feedback: Regularly seek feedback from colleagues, supervisors, and subordinates to gain different perspectives and identify areas for improvement. Use feedback constructively to enhance your adaptability skills.

Develop Problem-Solving Skills: Enhance your problem-solving abilities by practicing critical thinking, analyzing complex situations, and developing creative solutions. Seek out opportunities to tackle challenging problems and learn from the experience.

Cultivate Emotional Intelligence: Develop self-awareness and emotional regulation skills to manage emotions and respond positively to change effectively. This helps create a supportive and adaptable work environment.

How to Highlight Adaptability Skills:

When showcasing your adaptability skills in resumes, interviews, or performance evaluations, consider the following strategies:

Share Specific Examples: Provide concrete examples of situations where you demonstrated adaptability. Describe the challenges faced, the actions taken, and the positive outcomes achieved.

Highlight Learning Experiences: Emphasize instances where you sought new learning opportunities or proactively acquired new skills to adapt to changing circumstances.

Discuss Collaboration and Teamwork: Demonstrate how you collaborated with colleagues, shared ideas, and worked together to overcome challenges. Highlight your ability to adapt your communication style to work effectively with different individuals.

Show Problem-Solving Abilities: Describe how you approached complex problems, analyzed them from different angles, and developed creative solutions. Explain the positive impact of your problem-solving skills on the organization.

Adaptability in the workplace is essential for several reasons:

Dealing with Change: The business landscape constantly evolves, with new technologies, market trends, and customer expectations emerging. Adaptability enables individuals and organizations to navigate change successfully.

Embracing Innovation: Adaptable employees and managers are more likely to embrace innovative ideas and approaches. They are open to experimenting with new strategies and technologies, leading to increased efficiency and competitiveness.

Facing Challenges: Adaptable individuals can effectively handle challenges and setbacks. They remain resilient, maintain a positive attitude, and find solutions to overcome obstacles, fostering a culture of problem-solving within the organization.

Enhancing Employee Engagement and Satisfaction: Employees who feel supported in adapting to change experience higher engagement and job satisfaction. They feel valued and empowered to contribute their ideas and skills to the organization's success.

Driving Organizational Agility: Adaptability is a key driver of organizational agility, which is the ability to respond quickly and effectively to changing market conditions. Agile organizations are better equipped to seize opportunities, stay ahead of competitors, and thrive in dynamic environments.

Promoting Innovation and Creativity: Adaptability encourages a culture of innovation and creativity. When employees are open to change and willing to explore new ideas, they are more likely to contribute innovative solutions and drive continuous improvement within the organization.

Building a Resilient Workforce: An adaptable workforce is inherently more resilient. When individuals and teams can adjust to new challenges and bounce back from setbacks, they maintain high productivity and motivation, even in the face of adversity.

How to Become More Adaptable at Work:

Develop a Growth Mindset: Embrace a mindset that sees change as an opportunity for growth and learning. Believe in your ability to acquire new skills and adapt to new circumstances.

Stay Curious and Informed: Stay updated with industry trends, technological advancements, and best practices. Seek out learning opportunities and stay curious about new developments in your field.

Build a Strong Network: Surround yourself with diverse individuals with different perspectives and experiences. Engage in meaningful conversations and learn from others' insights.

Practice Flexibility: Be open to new ideas and approaches. Adapt your plans and strategies when necessary and be willing to let go of old ways of doing things.

Develop Emotional Intelligence: Enhance your emotional intelligence by becoming more self-aware and developing empathy for others. This allows you to manage your emotions effectively and navigate change-related stress.

Seek Feedback and Learn from Mistakes: Actively seek feedback from others and learn from your mistakes. View setbacks as opportunities for growth and identify areas for improvement.

Adaptability is a vital skill in today's ever-changing workplace. It enables individuals and organizations to navigate new challenges and trends effectively. Managers can stay responsive and proactive in the face of change by embracing a growth mindset, fostering a learning culture, and developing adaptability skills. Cultivating adaptability leads to a more resilient workforce and promotes innovation, problem-solving, and organizational agility. By prioritizing adaptability, managers can create a thriving and dynamic work environment that positions their teams and organizations for long-term success.

Chapter Summary and Key Takeaways:

In Chapter 7, we explored the crucial role of driving change and addressing modern leadership challenges. We underlined the significance of change management in the present-day business world, showcasing how a systematic approach can lead to increased productivity, better decision-making, and a positive work environment. This goes hand in hand with employing effective strategies for leading change, be it through clear vision articulation, involving employees in the process, or using popular change management models.

We also underscored the need for adaptability in the face of new trends and challenges, stressing how flexibility and resilience can equip leaders to better handle workplace dynamics. Real-life stories from leaders served as practical examples to understand the challenges and how to overcome them.

But as we delve deeper into the realm of leadership, one thing becomes apparent: the success of any leader is intimately tied to their level of self-confidence. It's this confidence that allows leaders to inspire others, make tough decisions, and navigate the unknown. However, self-doubt can creep in and hamper even the best leaders.

As we transition to Chapter 8, "Boosting Self-Confidence and Overcoming Self-Doubt," we'll examine the interplay between confidence and self-doubt in a leader's journey. We'll offer strategies to foster self-confidence and tools to counter self-doubt, allowing leaders to fully utilize their potential. From understanding the impact of self-confidence on leadership effectiveness to learning how to rise above self-doubt, we'll continue to arm you with practical knowledge and skills essential for today's successful leadership. It's a journey that necessitates introspection and personal growth, but it's one well worth undertaking for those aiming to make a difference in their organization and team. So, let's dive into this critical aspect of leadership development in the next chapter.

CHAPTER 8
BOOSTING SELF-CONFIDENCE AND OVERCOMING SELF-DOUBT

> "Self-doubt can create fatigue in your mind, whereas focused action can create achievement in your life."
>
> JACKIE CANTONI

UNDERSTANDING IMPOSTER SYNDROME

What is imposter syndrome

Imposter syndrome is a psychological phenomenon in which people cannot internalize their accomplishments. Despite external evidence of their competence, those with the syndrome remain convinced that they are frauds and do not deserve the success they have achieved. Proof of success is dismissed as luck, timing, or as a result of deceiving others into thinking they are more intelligent and capable than they believe themselves to be.

People with imposter syndrome have very fragile self-esteem; even minor criticism can lead them to believe they are worthless or a complete failure. Imposter syndrome is reported among successful or well-known people in any area of social life. It affects an individual's understanding of ability, intelligence, and accomplishments. This can be exemplified in a person's attempt to attribute their success to luck rather than talent, fear that others may not perceive them differently from others, or an inability to recognize what they have contributed to the work.

It is often brought on when people feel that they are not recognized for their accomplishments and can be triggered by external factors such as low salary increases or even a failure at a previous place of work.

What causes imposter syndrome

Psychologists have found that imposter syndrome is often caused by uncertainty about self-worth. This can be triggered by the public's opinion and perceived lack of esteem, leading to questioning one's intelligence, skills, or competence. This can be seen in people who are terrified at the prospect of facing a professional interview or just after a successful presentation.

Imposter syndrome can also stem from the fear that people will question your ability to do your job and that you will lose it all. Imposter syndrome can be prevalent among women who feel they might not be as good as their male counterparts or have been passed over for a promotion or raise. Generally, people with imposter syndrome seek validation and acknowledgment of their abilities.

Characteristics of imposter syndrome

Imposter syndrome is characterized by insecure self-esteem, fears of being exposed as fraudulent or incompetent, and general discomfort when meeting new people.

Imposter Syndrome manifests in various ways, and individuals experiencing it may display the following characteristics:

a) Persistent self-doubt: Individuals with Imposter Syndrome constantly question their abilities and competence, despite external evidence suggesting otherwise.

b) Fear of failure: There is a deep-seated fear of failure or making mistakes. People with Imposter Syndrome often set excessively high standards for themselves, fearing that any minor misstep will expose them as frauds.

c) Discounting achievements: They downplay or dismiss their accomplishments, attributing them to luck, timing, or other external factors. They struggle to internalize their successes.

d) Overworking: People with Imposter Syndrome may overcompensate for their inadequacy by working excessively hard, striving for perfection in every task, and seeking external validation.

Types of imposter syndrome

Imposter Syndrome can manifest in different ways, and individuals may identify with one or more of the following types:

- **The Perfectionist:** Perfectionists set exceedingly high standards for themselves and fear making mistakes. They believe that anything less than perfection is a failure.
- **The Expert:** Experts need to know everything before starting a task or project. They constantly seek more knowledge and skills, fearing not knowing enough.

- **The Natural Genius:** Natural geniuses believe intelligence and skills should come effortlessly. They feel ashamed and incompetent when they struggle or need to put in the effort.
- **The Soloist:** Soloists prefer to work alone and avoid asking for help. They feel that asking for assistance would expose their lack of knowledge or abilities.
- **The Superhero:** Superheroes push themselves to do everything and do it flawlessly. They feel compelled to excel in every aspect of their lives and tend to neglect self-care.

What kind of imposter are you? 15 questions to help you find out

To determine the type of imposter syndrome you may be experiencing, reflect on the following questions:

- Do you set excessively high standards for yourself?
- Do you struggle with asking for help or delegating tasks?
- Do you feel like you must excel in all areas of your work or life?
- Do you worry that you will be exposed as a fraud?

- Do you attribute your success to luck or external factors?
- Do you downplay or dismiss compliments or positive feedback?
- Do you fear making mistakes or failing?
- Do you feel a constant pressure to prove your competence?
- Do you believe things would come easily to you if you were competent?
- Do you often compare yourself to others and feel inadequate as a result?
- Do you feel uncomfortable acknowledging your achievements?
- Do you hesitate to share your opinions or ideas for fear of being judged?
- Do you feel a constant pressure to prove your competence?
- Do you believe things would come easily to you if you were competent?
- Do you often compare yourself to others and feel inadequate as a result?
- Do you feel uncomfortable acknowledging your achievements?
- Do you hesitate to share your opinions or ideas for fear of being judged?

How to deal with Imposter Syndrome

There are a few things that you can do to help overcome imposter syndrome and build self-confidence.

The first step to overcoming imposter syndrome is admitting that it is real. Many people feel they cannot succeed because they believe their successes were based on luck and are convinced, they will fail again. Believing this can cause negative feelings of worthlessness and the inability to let go of the previous failure, which will then lead to developing imposter syndrome. It's important to recognize the emotional roots of imposter syndrome so that you can root out the issue causing it.

Next, it is highly important that you set realistic goals and values. Setting unrealistic goals and higher-than-normal expectations can lead to the development of imposter syndrome. It is important to set reasonable expectations for self-improvement and know that success is an organic process where failure is an ever-present possibility. Life's reality does not mean you will fail, so you must use self-compassion and patience as you build toward your goals. In addition, setting high standards causes stress due to perfectionism, which exacerbates imposter syndrome.

If you feel the effects of imposter syndrome, it is important to talk to someone you feel comfortable with and can trust. Expressing your feelings is the first step in overcoming this debilitating condition. Although it may be difficult for you to admit, most people have felt like an imposter at some point in their lives, and by talking about it, you will be able to gain an empathetic perspective of others' experiences with imposter syndrome and build self-worth.

Additionally, it's important not to compare yourself with others because that can only lead to feelings of inadequacy. One thing that will keep imposter syndrome in check is celebrating your successes as they come without taking them for granted. This is because most people's success is built upon years of hard work and love for what they do. Celebrating your victories, no matter how small, may be helpful by writing them down in a journal or on social media. By identifying your hard work and celebrating your victories, you will realize that success isn't accidental; it's the result of hard work and perseverance.

Finally, it's important to practice self-care because although imposter syndrome can cause burnout and feelings of inadequacy, it can also lead to depression and anxiety. Seeking help through therapy will help you learn how to overcome feelings of inadequacy caused by imposter syndrome.

Bias and imposter syndrome

Imposter syndrome is not a gender-specific issue; it affects people of all races, gender expressions, sexual orientations, and age groups. Imposter syndrome afflicts both men and women in almost equal measure. Despite increasing awareness of experiences with imposter syndrome, it is often difficult to admit that one suffers from the condition. Even though women tend to experience imposter syndrome at a slightly higher rate than men, it is important to acknowledge that men are not immune from the effects of imposter syndrome even if they tend to feel undeserving or less deserving of their achievements vis-à-vis their female counterparts. Although imposter syndrome is prevalent, it is not necessarily more common than other psychological and emotional disorders, such as bipolar disorder.

Imposter syndrome could potentially be a problem in terms of workplace bias. Many people believe that women who feel like imposters are less confident in their abilities to complete tasks as well as their male counterparts, which could make them less likely to be promoted or advanced within a company or corporation.

Though this may be true for some people, it's important to note that many women tend to undervalue their work and capabilities since they are often the ones who are raising children and taking care of the home. Their career accomplishments can often be attributed to this reality versus experiences with imposter syndrome.

Recognizing and addressing bias within oneself is important to prevent possible issues from arising in the workplace. However, it is also important to acknowledge that this is only one small part of a larger picture and does not validate all imposter syndrome instances as discriminatory against women. In some cases, bias may be a factor, but in other cases, it can be assumed that men and women are experiencing imposter syndrome for different reasons.

In addition to the negative effects felt by people suffering from imposter syndrome, numerous benefits derive from recognizing and learning how to combat the condition through self-awareness. Since people with imposter syndrome tend to undervalue their abilities, they are often more open to self-improvement or development than those who do not have the condition.

9 Ways to Overcome Imposter Syndrome

Imposter syndrome is characterized by feelings of intellectual fraudulence and the fear that others will discover this. Feeling like an imposter will hold you back from accomplishing your goals because of the negative thoughts it instills in you. Consider these strategies to help you conquer impostor syndrome and achieve success:

a) Understand that imposter syndrome is a real condition with a name. Instead of using the word "impostor" as a form of self-deprecation, identify it as "imposter syndrome."

b) Understand that impostor syndrome is not simply a mental disorder but a medical condition. Being open to your feelings and honest will help you overcome this disease.

c) Understand that what you are experiencing is not your fault. For example, they become anxious when speaking in front of groups or don't complete tasks on time. There may be underlying causes for these feelings, such as not receiving enough attention growing up or not feeling like you were successful at achieving goals because of competition.

d) Understand that you are not a fraud, a loser, or an impostor. Instead, you are simply experiencing feelings of inadequacy due to normal human development.

e) Do not compare yourself to others. Everyone has different traits and experiences, making us unique and special.

f) Practice self-love by celebrating your successes regularly. Dedicate time each day to reflect on your accomplishments and how fortunate the world is to have someone like you!

g) Accepting the fact that there is help for this condition through therapy is important to overcoming imposter syndrome because it helps people gain control over their negative thoughts and feelings associated with this condition.

h) Understand that you cannot control other people's thoughts, feelings, or actions. However, you can help yourself feel more confident in your abilities by acknowledging what you are good at, identifying your strengths, and knowing that while imposter syndrome is real, it will not hold you back from achieving success.

Conquer imposter syndrome with confidence!

Imposter syndrome is a complex disorder that can be described as an anxiety condition based on the feeling of being a fraud. It has been linked to negative thoughts, feelings, and behaviors. There are many possible causes of imposter syndrome, but it is important to know that it will not make you fail while you are pursuing your goals and dreams. Please take comfort in the fact that there are people out there who are living with this pill and working through their problems every single day.

Imposter syndrome causes people to feel unqualified or inadequate, which is why a lot of times, they will choose not to apply for jobs or internships. It is also common for students and workers with imposter syndrome to avoid networking opportunities, making friends, and openly discussing their accomplishments. But by not speaking up, you are letting your imposter syndrome win, so you must start speaking up about your achievements.

Overcoming Imposter Syndrome is a journey that requires self-reflection, self-compassion, and adopting positive strategies. You can build resilience and confidence in your abilities by recognizing achievements, challenging negative thoughts, seeking support, and fostering a positive work environment. Remember, you are not alone in experiencing Imposter Syndrome, and with perseverance and self-belief, you can overcome it and reach your full potential. Embrace your talents, celebrate your successes, and continue to learn and grow.

BUILDING SELF-CONFIDENCE IN YOURSELF AND YOUR TEAM

The Critical Connection Between Confidence and Leadership

Confidence is essential to leadership; leaders must have high confidence levels to propel their organization forward. However, this also means that leaders need to understand the challenges of dealing with imposter syndrome within their organizations because if they do not recognize and address these challenges, it can harm their ability to connect with an effective and motivated workforce. Imposter syndrome can be defined as a condition that causes some people to feel inadequate about their abilities.

This connection between confidence and leadership is just as, if not more, important in business than the connection between confidence and success. People with high confidence levels tend to make better leaders than those without. This means that leaders with high confidence levels tend to have more successful careers and build stronger businesses because they can lead teams with confidence in themselves and each other.

Imposter syndrome can have a negative effect on the organization. People affected by imposter syndrome are likelier to choose not to apply for jobs if they do not feel qualified or worthy of the position. This can be detrimental because new talent is crucial to growing businesses and organizations. When people believe that there is someone else better for the job, it can cause them to either lose motivation or be less productive in their current positions, which has a negative impact on the entire business.

How to Build Confidence in Yourself and Your Leadership

Confidence is vital to leadership because it helps attract talent and motivate your team. It can be difficult for people to build self-confidence, especially if they do not feel good enough to lead. However, leaders with high confidence levels are more likely to be successful because they can connect with motivated teams that believe in them and their abilities.

There are many ways that you can help yourself gain more confidence in yourself and make yourself a better leader. By doing these simple things, you will become more confident and feel as though you have the skills necessary to lead your business or organization well:

a) **Recognize that you are a leader.** Accept that you have the skills and knowledge to effectively lead your team and organization.

b) List your strengths, talents, accomplishments, and special qualities. Studies show that the more strengths you identify within yourself, the greater your self-confidence will be!

c) Identify your weaknesses and take steps to improve these areas. Work on things that need improvement because they will help to boost your confidence levels.

d) Work on your communication and networking skills. Working under the assumption that you are a fraud can make it hard to connect with people, but if you build your communication skills, you can get your message across more effectively and build relationships with influential people in the industry.

e) Take steps to improve yourself. Identify areas that need improvement and take steps to grow in these areas. Being proactive will help you grow as a leader and know that no matter what happens, you have the skills necessary to deal with the challenges.

f) Get rid of negative thoughts about yourself. When improving your self-confidence, keeping negative thoughts out of your mind is important. By doing this, you will be more likely to feel confident in yourself and not feel as though you are a fraud.

g) Set goals for yourself and your team. Knowing that your team has goals for the year, or even the quarter or month, will help keep everyone motivated and working towards success.

h) Take a moment to appreciate yourself, no matter how small it is. Taking ourselves and our achievements for granted is easy, but always making time to thank yourself can boost your confidence. Work on self-love because when you work on loving yourself, you will also be more confident in leading others and connecting with them.

i) Make sure you are also positive about other people's achievements. Recognize that others had the same experiences as you did and worked hard for their accomplishments. Being positive about other people's achievements will help you feel more confident as a leader.

j) Show appreciation for others' work. When speaking to other people about their accomplishments, stay positive and highlight the good aspects of their work, even if you disagree with everything they have done or accomplished. This will help boost your confidence levels and make it easier to build connections with them.

k) Create places where you can connect with other people that are working towards the same goals as you are.

The benefits of confidence

The benefits of cultivating confidence in yourself are abundant. These positive traits and characteristics will help you connect with others and will help you gain the skills necessary for being a successful leader.

1. One of the main benefits of being confident is that it puts you in a position to do great things. Feeling confident in yourself allows you to take risks and read situations that may not have been clear to others. When you feel this way, it is easier for others to feel secure around you because they know your words are genuine, not just empty promises.

2. Having confidence in yourself can also reduce stress levels, which can be vital to leadership because stress is one of the biggest obstacles to achieving corporate success. By being confident in yourself and your leadership, you can focus on the important aspects of your job without constantly thinking that you are not up to the task.

3. Confidence can also help build self-esteem. When people feel good about themselves, they are more likely to be successful because they are happier with themselves and will be able to focus on things that matter instead of focusing on their mistakes.

4. You Will Feel More Secure When Leading

Confidence is essential for leaders because it helps them connect with others better and gives them a general sense of security in their professional lives. This trait will make you feel more secure with yourself and everything you do. Without confidence, it is easy to become scared of taking risks and make mistakes in speaking to people. When you feel confident in yourself, you will feel that nothing can hold you back and that nothing can stop you from achieving your goals.

5. You Will Have More Communication Skills

One of the biggest problems for leaders when communicating with others is feeling unclear about what they want or need to know. Confidence allows leaders to speak more effectively because they know what they want others to hear. Confidence also allows leaders to help other people better understand their thoughts and feelings by speaking about their feelings more sensitively than most people would without confidence.

6. People Will Want to Work With You

Building a team around you is one of the most crucial aspects of having success in your career. People will want to work with you because they will feel you are approachable and can talk to you about any concerns they may have. When leaders feel confident in themselves, they can easily connect with others on a more personal level, making it easier for people to work together without feeling uncomfortable and having difficulty talking with their bosses.

When people see that you are confident in yourself, they will be more likely to trust your decisions and take your word as true.

What Confident People Do

Confidence is a trait that many people have, but not all are confident in their ability to be confident. Confident people have the following traits:

1. *They Know What They Want*

Confident people know what they want from life and what they want from other people. They know exactly what they do and do not want from other people and can speak about these things so that others understand them.

Confident people also know what they need; when the need arises, they can turn to other friends, family members, or coworkers for help.

2. They Do Not Compromise Their Values

Confident people can identify their values and how much value each has on them. They are not willing to compromise their values and change how they see things to fit in with the rest of society or others.

3. They Do Not Change Their Minds Easily

Confident people know what they want from life and are not willing to accept anything less than that. This means that when you tell them something, they will believe it because it is what they have chosen to believe. They would rather stick to their guns on a topic than comply with your request because it does not match what they feel is right and true.

4. They Are Not Afraid to Take Risks

Confident people know how to take risks when opportunities arise. They do not shy away from new opportunities and anything that makes them feel scared or uneasy because they have to grow as people and explore new things happening in the world.

5. They Know When to Ask for Help

Confident people know when to ask others for help and can come up with solutions without feeling burdening other people. Confidence means knowing when you need help, not asking for it, but knowing that you can ask other people for assistance if the situation calls for it.

6. They Are Comfortable With The Way That They Are

Confident people know how they look, what they think, what they feel, and their opinions on different topics. They are comfortable with their identity and do not try to change themselves to fit in with others.

7. They Do Not Judge Others

Confident people do not judge based on how they look, talk, or think. They can accept everyone for who they are and have no problem being friends with people who may be different.

8. They Do Not Give Up Easily

Confident people know how hard it is to build a life for themselves and will do everything possible to see their goals through without letting obstacles get in their way.

On Leadership and Confidence and Self-Efficacy:

The role of confidence in leadership is often underestimated and is not given enough attention by researchers and practitioners. This leads to management theories that do not properly consider the impact of confidence on effective leadership, resulting in relatively limited benefits. One recent and noteworthy development in this area is the study of the relationship between leadership skills and self-efficacy. Leaders do not necessarily need to be confident but must believe they can perform well when faced with demanding challenges. Self-efficacy is a primary mediator explaining the relationship between leaders' self-confidence and job performance. It does so by measuring a leader's ability to influence outcomes and perceiving such influence as effective.

Confidence can also be defined as a leader's belief in their ability to achieve success or effectiveness. Thus, leaders with high self-efficacy are generally more confident in their skills and abilities. In this way, self-efficacy and confidence play a crucial role in leadership development and have been identified as key determinants of school leadership effectiveness by many international researchers.

Ways to instill confidence in your team members

Confidence is a skill that can be taken and learned by all people in many different situations. You must learn how to build confidence in all situations, not just workplace ones; however, as a manager or someone who works with people daily, this is the most likely situation you will face. By using some of the methods listed below, you can provide your employees with the confidence they need so they can work more effectively and meet your goals:

a) Provide Challenging Assignments:

If your employees fear stepping out of the box, you might want to try giving them more challenging positions. In this case, they will feel that they can do it and will feel more comfortable wearing a cape.

Creating an environment that stimulates everyone is key to making this great. For example, if you notice that your employees tend not to volunteer much or make new connections with other people outside of the normal workplace process, make an effort to host social events where team members can meet new people. This is also a great way to give employees access to customer-based areas as they can interact with them in a friendly way.

b) Provide Opportunities for Growth and Experience:

One of the biggest bottlenecks when it comes to confidence is self-imposed limitations. If you have an employee who isn't confident in their leadership skills, you might have to give them more opportunities to make mistakes while still supervised. Allowing them more time allows them to make a few mistakes and learn from them instead of being scared away because of their previous experience. When this happens, they will gradually gain greater confidence in their abilities, boosting their self-efficacy.

c) Give Constructive Feedback:

Ask employees to give you honest but constructive feedback. If they are not confident in their work, it will be easy to see it in their work and speak out about it. However, sometimes people might be scared to do this because they feel they will be seen as having no skill or ability. If you haven't ever dealt with something like this before, then let your employee know that you want them to show their ability and come up with an idea of how they can do better.

*d) **Give Positive Reassurance:***

Sometimes, people are afraid to speak up and ask for help. If you see this in your employees, then take the initiative to reassure them that you will help them. This is a great way to build their confidence, and they will feel supported in their work.

*e) **Have a Positive Environment:***

A lot of people get intimidated in the workplace by a negative environment. You might consider changing things when employees feel they can't breathe or be themselves.

One of the best ways for this is by creating an environment where everyone feels comfortable being themselves and different people have different ways of expressing themselves. When you do this, you can show your employees that they don't have to feel like they have to be serious all the time and that they have a great sense of humor.

*f) **Be a Good Example:***

For employees to feel confident, they need to know that their manager is capable and willing to accept them.

You can best do this by being open about your mistakes and the mistakes you see in others. Showing the human side to yourself will allow others to feel more comfortable in what they are doing and more confident about themselves.

LEVERAGING FEAR FOR PERSONAL AND PROFESSIONAL GROWTH

The Science Behind Fear

Fear is a powerful emotion that can be exploited for personal and professional growth. Fear of failure, fear of success, and fear of not meeting others' expectations are all emotions that can be used to spur personal and professional growth when used effectively.

1) Be aware of the power of fear in your life:

The most fundamental way to gain awareness of how fear impacts our lives is by being honest about how we feel about different situations. Knowing how we feel about things such as rejection or possible failure, for example, gives us a better idea about how we will react to these things and what we need to do to prevent personally overwhelming outcomes.

2) Identify the underlying reason for the fear:

Once we acknowledge our fear of a situation, an important next step is identifying the underlying reason. It may simply be that our fear of something is because of how we perceive others or how they may judge us. It also might be that we are afraid of failure because we believe that if we fail, it will reflect badly on our skills. Understanding why and identifying what you are afraid of can help develop strategies to deal with this fear.

3) Be honest with yourself about how you feel:

It is very important, to be honest with yourself and not try to sugarcoat your emotions. When we sugar-coat our emotions, we may be able to manage them for the short term and trick ourselves into feeling like everything is okay, but in the long term, it will still come out as a negative emotion. By being honest with ourselves about our feelings, we can build strategies to deal with these emotions more effectively.

4) Start to take measured steps toward the things that you are afraid of:

The fourth step is to start taking measured steps toward the things you fear. It is very important that when we do start taking these steps, they should be small and manageable. Trying to jump in head-first will make us more likely to give up because of how overwhelming the situation seems. Doing this step slowly and identifying small incremental growth opportunities will make it much easier for us to stay on track and push ourselves through these situations more effectively.

5) *Look for opportunities to challenge yourself:*

Finally, we need to start looking for opportunities to challenge ourselves. These opportunities should be specific, challenging, and measurable. They should be challenging because they will present us with outcomes we don't want and give us a chance to grow and improve. These challenges should be quantified to measure our progress in overcoming them. The more measurable they are, the easier for us to track our progress and know what is working versus what isn't.

The science behind fear lies in its ability to activate the amygdala, the part of the brain responsible for processing emotions. A part of the brain called the hippocampus also plays a role in processing emotions by recalling memories similar to the current situation. Thus, when we experience fear stimulates these two parts of the brain and leads us to react with fight or flight responses. In other words, fear is a physiological response that allows us to experience danger which can trigger both mental and physical reactions, including increased heart rate, sweating, etc. As with all emotions, there is a positive use for fear as well as negative use for fear.

Fear can catalyze building confidence and competence. When individuals confront their fears, they gain a sense of accomplishment and become more self-assured. By facing fears, individuals may see that their fears are not as bad as they seem and that the situation is manageable. Research has also shown that individuals who have faced their fears are more likely to see future tasks as less overwhelming or worrisome.

Fear has been shown to cause a physiological reaction that activates an important biological mechanism. This mechanism prepares a person for self-defense by increasing blood pressure, heart rate, and alertness through the secretion of adrenaline.

Adrenaline is responsible for increasing reactions such as motor output and muscle tension. As individuals react to fear, they gain more experience in confronting potentially threatening situations and become better at dealing with them in the future.

The Positive Side of Fear - 15 Benefits of Fear:

The provided Thrive yard article highlights various benefits of embracing fear:

1. Heightened Awareness: Fear sharpens your senses and increases awareness of potential risks or dangers.
2. Acknowledgment and Enlightenment: Facing fear allows individuals to acknowledge their vulnerabilities and better understand themselves.
3. Focus and Concentration: Fear narrows the focus, allowing individuals to concentrate on the task.
4. Preparation and Planning: Fear prompts individuals to prepare and plan for potential challenges or threats.
5. Choices, Analysis, and Evaluation: Fear forces individuals to assess their options and make informed decisions.
6. Dissecting Extremes: Fear helps individuals analyze extreme outcomes and consider the possibilities in between.
7. Removal of Barriers: Fear can push individuals to break through mental and emotional barriers that hinder progress.

8. Breaking Routine: Fear encourages individuals to leave their comfort zones and embrace new experiences.
9. Opportunities and Resource Identification: Fear can lead individuals to identify opportunities and resources they may have overlooked.
10. Activates Championship Mentality: Fear can ignite a competitive spirit and drive individuals to perform at their best.
11. Motivates You to Build Skills: Fear motivates individuals to acquire new skills and knowledge to overcome challenges.
12. Letting Go and the 'After-strength': Confronting fear allows individuals to experience relief and build resilience.
13. Overcoming Fear and Reward Anticipation: Successfully overcoming fear can generate a sense of accomplishment and anticipation for future rewards.
14. Replicating the Breakthroughs: By conquering one fear, individuals gain confidence in overcoming other obstacles.
15. Helping Others Overcome Their Fears: Individuals who have faced and conquered their fears can inspire and support others on their journeys.

Ways to Think Differently About Fear

We must understand and accept that fear is a part of our lives and be equipped to deal with it. Below are some questions you can ask yourself when fear strikes:

Why is this fear of mine happening? Do I feel slightly uncomfortable before I am ready? What situations or what people are causing me to feel this way? Can I test these possibilities before they occur by taking small steps in a controlled environment? Is there something I can do to make the situation better if it does occur?

Alain de Botton said, "People believe in love at first sight because they know from experience that what they once loved can never be the same again. This is because love depends on newness. It's like a piece of fruit that is always fresh and lovely, never the same twice."

When we feel frightened by something new, fresh, and unfamiliar, we can learn from this experience. If we become too fearful to face our new experiences, they will pass us by, leaving us with regret.

Fear is part of life for everyone. However, practicing deep breathing during fear or anxiety can help calm your mind. You won't have to fight your emotions but instead use them as a tool to help relieve the tension in your body. The more you practice deep breathing, the better you will get at taking control of your emotions and reducing feelings of anxiety and distress.

Fear can be useful in helping us learn new skills or get stronger in the case of athletics or other competitive endeavors. The more you face your fears, the more you will overcome them and be able to achieve your goals. If fear seems impossible, break it down into smaller steps, such as saying, "I'll just try to do one thing at a time."

Even though fear is meant to warn us about potential danger, it can be overdone and result in negative emotions. When you worry about something before it happens, you may find yourself trapped by your thoughts and become impatient with others when they don't happen as quickly as you want.

Fear can be used as a tool for communication in creative ways. If you fear public speaking, you can use it to your advantage by creating a new persona better suited to the situation. For example, if you fear public speaking but enjoy writing poetry, you could use your fear to create poetry as an outlet for expressing yourself in more creative ways.

Therefore, we are taught to always keep our fears under control through imagination and playing tricks on ourselves. This way, we can prevent worry, stress, and other such emotions that may make us angry or impatient with others.

Chapter Summary and Key Takeaways:

As we round off Chapter 8, we've delved deep into the realm of self-confidence, exploring its profound impact on effective leadership and its correlation with overcoming self-doubt. We started by understanding the phenomenon of Imposter Syndrome, a psychological pattern where individuals doubt their own accomplishments. With actionable strategies and insights, we've discussed how to recognize, confront, and overcome this issue, thereby fostering a positive work environment that encourages open communication and mutual support.

Next, we turned our focus on developing self-confidence, not just in ourselves but also within our teams. From leveraging individual strengths to nurturing a growth mindset and setting achievable goals, we underscored the value of constructive feedback and the significance of leading by example to instill confidence in our teams.

Lastly, we recognized the paradoxical power of fear as a tool for personal and professional growth. We acknowledged that fear, while commonly perceived as a negative emotion, can indeed serve as a compelling motivator, pushing us out of our comfort zones, encouraging us to overcome challenges, and ultimately fueling our resilience.

In essence, by mastering these skills and adopting these strategies, leaders can cultivate an atmosphere of confidence and authenticity, inspiring their team to reach greater heights of achievement.

SHARE THE SKILLS

As you set forward on the path to successful leadership, you're in a unique position to hold the door open for someone else.

Simply by sharing your honest opinion of this book and your leadership journey so far, you'll show new readers where they can find the guidance they need to excel in their own role.

MAKE A LASTING IMPRESSION!

Thank you for your support. A mark of a great leader is their willingness to help others to succeed.

CONCLUSION

In this remarkable exploration of the facets of leadership, we have journeyed together through the complexities, subtleties, and the transformative power of effective management. This book has been designed as a comprehensive guide, with each chapter offering insights and actionable strategies on various aspects of leadership. It is not just a reading experience, but a tool, intended to empower both existing and aspiring leaders with the knowledge, perspective, and techniques to elevate their leadership abilities to new heights.

Throughout this narrative, we have underscored the immense significance of communication, an attribute that lies at the very heart of successful leadership. We've delved into its importance, the different forms it can take, and how it can be utilized to build stronger relationships within your team. Good leaders don't just speak; they listen, they understand, and they inspire.

In the chapters on trust and integrity, we emphasized their role as the bedrock of any successful team. Without trust, there can be no genuine teamwork, and without integrity, there can be no lasting leadership. We have highlighted how these attributes can be fostered and upheld, not just within ourselves but also within the teams that we lead.

We further explored the concepts of delegation and coaching, key elements that drive team growth and development. By understanding how to effectively delegate tasks and responsibilities, leaders can empower their teams, leading to higher productivity, job satisfaction, and team morale. Simultaneously, through coaching, leaders can play an instrumental role in guiding their team members towards their personal and professional growth.

The discussion on self-confidence and overcoming self-doubt underscored that leaders are not immune to human insecurities. By addressing imposter syndrome, we provided strategies to enhance self-confidence. We embraced the idea that fear, instead of being a hindrance, can be a powerful motivator for personal and professional growth.

As we culminated with resilience, we consolidated the understanding that leadership involves navigating through uncertain and challenging circumstances. We championed the value of resilience, demonstrating how leaders can foster this quality within their teams to tackle difficulties head-on.

The principles and strategies we've discussed throughout this book are not theoretical constructs, but real, pragmatic solutions derived from years of research, observation, and experience. It's embodied in the success story of the XYZ company, where they turned around their fortune by embracing these leadership principles. The company moved from a struggling enterprise to a thriving one, their success a testament to the power of effective leadership.

Now, the baton is passed to you. It's time to put these principles into practice. Take your leadership skills to the next level. Learn, grow, and evolve into the kind of leader your team will respect, admire, and aspire to become. This book is not just about achieving results, it's about nurturing relationships, inspiring potential, and creating an enduring impact.

Remember, effective leadership is not a destination but a journey. It's about continually learning, adapting, and implementing new strategies for the betterment of your team, your organization, and ultimately, yourself. So, take action. Start implementing these proven strategies and become the best leader you can be. Your team, your company, and your career success depend on it.

As we conclude this journey, we hope that you found value in this exploration of leadership and that you feel equipped with new knowledge and strategies to enhance your leadership prowess. We would greatly appreciate if you would share your thoughts and experiences of reading this book. Please consider leaving a review to let us know what you've found most helpful, or what resonated the most with you.

Together, let's foster a world of empowered, inspiring, and compassionate leaders. The journey to effective leadership starts with a single step. Take that step today.

REFERENCES

Bass, B. M., & Riggio, R. E. (2006). Transformational leadership (2nd ed.). Psychology Press.

Blanchard, K., & Hodges, P. (2005). The servant leader: Transforming your heart, head, hands, and habits. Thomas Nelson.

Covey, S. R. (2013). The 7 habits of highly effective people: Powerful lessons in personal change. Simon & Schuster.

Drucker, P. F. (2008). The effective executive: The definitive guide to getting the right things done. HarperCollins.

Goleman, D., Boyatzis, R., & McKee, A. (2013). Primal leadership: Unleashing the power of emotional intelligence. Harvard Business Press.

Hackman, J. R., & Wageman, R. (2007). Asking the right questions about leadership: Discussion and conclusions. American Psychologist, 62(1), 43-47.

Heifetz, R., & Linsky, M. (2017). Leadership on the line: Staying alive through the dangers of leading. Harvard Business Review Press.

Kouzes, J. M., & Posner, B. Z. (2017). The leadership challenge: How to make extraordinary things happen in organizations (6th ed.). Jossey-Bass.

Kruse, K. (2012, October 16). *100 best quotes on leadership.* Forbes. https://www.forbes.com/sites/kevinkruse/2012/10/16/quotes-on-leadership/

Sinek, S. (2011). Start with why: How great leaders inspire everyone to take action. Penguin Group.

Yukl, G. (2012). Leadership in organizations (8th ed.). Pearson.

Made in the USA
Las Vegas, NV
15 December 2023